DiaGram

Language Support Pack

Diagnostic assessment and worksheets in grammar, punctuation and sentence-level skills

DiaGram

Language Support Pack

Diagnostic assessment and worksheets in grammar, punctuation and sentence-level skills

Adrienne Stevens

Hodder & Stoughton

A MEMBER OF THE HODDER HEADLINE GROUP

The author

Adrienne Stevens is a language and special needs tutor, and author of ***DiaPhon Diagnostic Phonics/Spelling Support Packs 1 & 2***. Her varied career includes teaching English to CSE/GCSE level in multi-racial comprehensive schools in socially deprived areas in the north and south of the country and a boy's Remand/Assessment Centre; teaching English as a second language; setting up and running a department for pupils with statements of special educational needs within a large comprehensive school; and work within the private sector of education. She holds an RSA Diploma in SpLD and is an active member of the Professional Association of Teachers of Students with Specific Learning Difficulties (PATOSS).

Acknowledgements

I would like to thank the teachers and pupils of Swanbourne House School, the Support Staff at Oundle School and my own pupils who have taken part in the development of ***DiaGram***. The positive response has been very encouraging.

Thank you, Charles Knight, for your wisdom, knowledge and support. I feel very fortunate to have a publisher whose judgement I trust and who is unfailingly courteous and decisive.

Time spent writing means time taken from family and friends. Thank you all for being so understanding and giving me space to complete this book.

The person who has kept me on-task throughout this project is my husband, John. Not only has he encouraged me to write but he has contributed ideas and written a first draft of some of the passages, to bring a male perspective to the content. Thank you. I wouldn't have done it without you.

Orders: please contact Bookpoint Ltd, 39 Milton Park, Abingdon, Oxon OX14 4TD. Telephone: (44) 01235 827720, Fax: (44) 01235 400454. Lines are open from 9.00 – 6.00, Monday to Saturday, with a 24 hour message answering service. Email address: orders@bookpoint.co.uk

British Library Cataloguing in Publication Data

A catalogue record for this title is available from The British Library

ISBN 0 340 79045 8
First published 2001
Impression number   10 9 8 7 6 5 4 3 2 1
Year   2005 2004 2003 2002 2001

Typeset by Dorchester Typesetting Group Ltd, Dorset.
Printed in Great Britain for Hodder & Stoughton Educational, a division of Hodder Headline Plc, 338 Euston Road, London NW1 3BH, by Hobbs the Printers, Totton, Hants.

Introduction

What is DiaGram?

The DiaGram Language Support Pack is a photocopiable resource which targets *knowledge of language* and the technical vocabulary relating to *parts of speech, punctuation* and the *effective use* of English.

DiaGram is intended for use with pupils following a Key Stage 3 programme of study who require specific teaching of points of grammar and knowledge of language. It is matched to core sentence-level teaching objectives of the National Literacy Strategy *Framework for Teaching English*, and is designed particularly to facilitate assessment, consolidation and 'quick and effective catch-up' at Year 7.

More than 60 **worksheets** target the key terms specified by the National Literacy Strategy, and provide a *definition* and/or *explanation*, with examples, plus *exercises* which provide opportunities for identifying each item in context and encourage pupils to produce their own examples. **Test sheets** enable the teacher to check whether or not pupils have grasped the formal terms used in discussion of both language and literature, and whether they can identify and apply that knowledge in a 'small steps' context. The tests may be administered *first* to see if work is required, or *after* completing the worksheets, to assess the extent to which pupils' understanding is secure. **Answers** to the tests and worksheets are provided.

A **diagnostic matrix** provides a 'contents' list, checklist and complete individual record of which areas have been taught and tested. The matrix makes planning for further teaching simple.

Failure to complete each test correctly will 'diagnose' a lack of knowledge. This identifies the need for further teaching/learning to take place before mastery of the topic can reasonably be assumed. **DiaGram** is thus particularly useful for pupils requiring learning support. The material can also be used as an extension pack with more able upper junior pupils and for revision by older pupils.

The way in which the material is used – whether as 'dip in' resource or structured programme – can be determined by the teacher and related to the age and ability of the pupils. Tests and worksheets can be used independently of each other if the teacher has a preference for his/her own teaching material. A sound knowledge of the meaning and application of this vocabulary can subsequently be exploited within a wider context of language and literature work.

DiaGram is intended to fulfil three main aims:

- to develop knowledge of the formal register of language used in discussion of English Language and English Literature, in order to support teaching through whole texts;
- to enable the teacher to assess quickly the extent of an individual pupil's knowledge of this vocabulary and its application;
- to provide teaching and assessment resources on parts of speech, punctuation and general knowledge of a register of language relating to the effective use of English.

Where appropriate, the standard dictionary abbreviations for parts of speech are given in the worksheets, which also form a set of revision notes.

How DiaGram works

The photocopiable **worksheets** can be used for individual, small-group and whole-class teaching. Most topics in the parts of speech and punctuation sections have a test page. Each **test** may be linked to one, two or more worksheets. The worksheet number(s) are indicated by the test reference – e.g. T1/3, T4, etc. The T refers to test and the numbers to the worksheets associated with the test sheet. The **diagnostic matrix** acts as a contents page for the worksheets and associated tests, and provides a complete record of progress.

Each test is followed by the name of the topic/sub-topics and the words *secure* and *work required*. A tick under the relevant heading is sufficient to record whether or not further action is required. In the context of **DiaGram**, *secure* is defined as there being no errors made in the identification and use of the target topics.

Once the teaching of the topic has taken place, complete the test and record the response. Where a test sheet is not available (e.g. for worksheets 18, 35, 45 and for the Special Effects section), the worksheet itself can be used as an indicator of the pupil's understanding of the language used and its application. If success is not achieved, both pupil and teacher know that a different approach to the problem is required and that more work must follow. It may require further explanation and examples from alternative sources. Time constraints will obviously limit the amount of teaching time available on any one topic. The focus on specific areas of difficulty, however, should help teachers plan their lessons with greater precision.

Intervention: using the worksheets

The **DiaGram** worksheets present information and exercises in small steps. Where relevant, the dictionary abbreviation for parts of speech is given in the text. A range of instructions is utilised as a means of building good study skills, whilst offering information and practice on the target topic. Both receptive and expressive work is included. Where space is provided for expressive work, opportunities for **diagnostic teaching** arise. This is useful in giving the teacher an **overview** of the pupil's general performance and highlighting areas of difficulty. It is also an opportunity for pupils to practise **proof reading skills**.

The worksheets are valuable resources as **homework** tasks. Individual needs can be met without using limited teaching time. The information included before each exercise will enable parents to become involved in supporting pupils at home. More able pupils will be able to follow the instructions with minimal supervision, leaving the teacher free to provide individual help to weaker members of the class.

The worksheets also build into a **reference and revision** resource for the pupil. Additional information can be inserted where topics are expanded as the pupil matures. For example, further work on verbs might include transitive/intransitive verbs. Work on sentence analysis would expand the depth of information on phrases and clauses.

Using the tests

Enter the pupil's name and date of test, and then ask the pupil simply to follow the instructions for the test. The instructions vary from test to test, and the discipline of reading and interpreting them accurately promotes good practice. Ask the pupil to work carefully but to move on to the next item in the test if he/she is unable to complete a question. When marking definitions of terms, allow any response which indicates an understanding of the term. Test numbering has been related to the worksheets.

Overview

DiaGram is a half-way house, building on work which has been presented, possibly in a simplified form, during earlier years. Subsequent work will make use of the sound base of knowledge in order to progress to a more detailed study of parts of speech, sentence analysis, fluent and varied writing of poetry and prose, confident, accurate speech and an understanding of the devices used by others in effective speech and writing.

The matrix provides a record of language which should be familiar to a pupil and is a useful source of information when a pupil moves from one class or school to another. It is invaluable in terms of target setting for mainstream pupils and preparing an individual education plan for pupils who are on the Special Educational Needs register.

Pupil response to this form of working has proved very positive. Teaching is made easier because the material is presented in such an accessible form and can be adapted to meet the needs of pupil and teacher. A working knowledge of parts of speech and the structure of verbs is very helpful for pupils learning a second language. The ability to identify by name, recognise in the work of others and utilise in expressive work, poetic devices and other forms of 'special effects', can only enhance every pupil's performance in English. **DiaGram** can help to achieve this aim.

Diagnostic Matrix

Class _____

Name _____

Parts of Speech	Work	Date	Test	Date		Work	Date	Test	Date	Special Effects	Work	Date	Test	Date
Simple sentences	1				Verbs – past tense	26				Paragraphs	50			
Compound sentences	2				Verbs – irregular past simple 1	27				Paragraphing	51		T50/1	
Complex sentences	3		T1/3		Verbs – irregular past simple 2	28				Similes	52			
Interrogatives & imperatives	4		T4		Verbs – p.perfect & p.perfect continuous	29				Metaphor	53			
Conjunctions	5				Verbs – future: simple & continuous	30				Alliteration, consonance & assonance	54			
Connectives	6		T5/6		Verbs – future perf. & f.perf. continuous	31		T23/31		Onomatopoeia	55			
Phrases & clauses	7		T7		Adverbs	32				Personification	56			
Common nouns & articles	8				Types of adverbs	33		T32/3		Synonyms & antonyms	57			
Proper nouns	9				Adverbs – compar./ superlative	34		T34		Homographs & homonyms	58			
Abstract nouns	10				Adverbs – spelling rules	35				Homophones	59			
Collective nouns	11		T8/11		Relative pronouns	36				Colloquial expressions	60			
Pronouns: subj/object	12				Pronouns – I & me	37		T36/7		Cliché & pun	61			
Types of pronouns	13		T12/13		Prepositions	38		T38		Rhythm & rhyme	62			
Singular & plural	14		T14		*Punctuation*					Repetition & exaggeration	63			
Adjectives – describing	15				Capital letters	39				Imported language	64			
Adjectives – comparing	16				Full stops	40		T39/40		Standard & non-standard English	65			
Adjectives – possession	17		T15/17		Commas	41		T41						
Finite & non-finite verbs	18				Apostrophe of omission	42								
Verbs – participles	19				Apostrophe of possession	43		T42/3						
Auxiliary verbs – to be & to have	20				Exclamation & question marks	44		T44						
Auxiliary verbs – to do	21		T20/1		Brackets	45								
Verbs – active & passive voices	22		T22		Hyphens & dashes	46		T46						
Verbs – tenses	23				Speech marks	47								
Verbs – present tense	24				Direct & indirect speech	48		T47/8						
Verbs – present perfect & perfect continuous.	25				Semi-colon & colon	49		T49						

DiaGram is published by Hodder & Stoughton Educational.
The publishers grant permission for photocopies of this sheet to be made for use solely in the purchasing institution.

Simple sentences

A **sentence** is a series of words which, when spoken or written, can stand alone and make sense. It is *always* written with a **capital letter** at the beginning and a **full stop** at the end.

A **simple sentence** expresses *one* idea and has *one* finite verb.
A **finite verb** has ***person*** (a subject which has a name, or a pronoun: *I, you, he, she, it, we, they*) and ***tense*** (*when* it takes place: see sheet 23).

> The **cat** (*subject*) **sat** (*verb, past tense*) on the mat.
> **I** (*subject*) **eat** (*verb, present tense*) lots of fruit and vegetables.

A simple sentence *can* consist of only one or two words. This is often a response to a *question*, a *command* or a *statement*. The punctuation is the same as in a longer sentence:

> 'Are you ready yet?'   'Be quick.'   'He's dead.'

Such sentences are usually spoken, but you may use them in written work to create an effect such as fear or urgency, or if you are writing direct speech:

> 'Get down!'   (= [You] get down!)
> 'Quiet!'   (= [You be] quiet!)

- -

Fill in the gaps in these simple sentences with one of these verbs:

cut   sings   play   cooked   watched   ran

1. I _____ my finger very badly.

2. Can you _____ the piano?

3. I _____ the television.

4. The boys _____ away shouting.

5. He _____ in a band.

6. Dad _____ the dinner today.

- -

Write some simple sentences of your own, using the starter words to help you.

1. The dog _____

2. My sister _____

3. Doctor _____

4. The mouse _____

5. I was _____

DiaGram is published by Hodder & Stoughton Educational.
The publishers grant permission for photocopies of this sheet to be made for use solely in the purchasing institution.

Compound sentences

DiaGram

Date _____

Name _____

Compound sentences have two or more ideas linked together by **conjunctions**:

> I went to the shops **and** John peeled the potatoes.
> We went to the concert hall **but** all the tickets were sold.

This is the most basic way of **joining** simple sentences or clauses (see sheet 7) together. In fact, you are putting two or more *equal* ideas together in one sentence. **Joining words** (conjunctions) such as *and, but* and *because* are used to link the parts together, but there are other forms of connectives (see sheet 6).

More joining words

    although   since   when   before   until   while   after   as   or   unless   then   if

---

Use conjunctions to join these short sentences together, to form one longer sentence. You may have to miss out or change some words and alter the order of others. The first one is done for you.

The lorry driver had a mate. The mate was asleep.
<u>The lorry driver had a mate **but** he was asleep.</u>

1. The boy kicked the tin can. He was walking to school.

   _____

2. The elephant ate the bananas. The elephant was hungry.

   _____

3. You can do the job now. You can do it tomorrow.

   _____

4. He can juggle with three balls. He can sing at the same time.

   _____

5. I washed the dishes happily. My mum promised me a treat.

   _____

6. I clean my teeth. I eat my breakfast.

   _____

7. You can come and see me now. You can come later.

   _____

8. I will play football. I can play in goal.

   _____

Complex sentences

Complex means 'made up of parts'. In a **complex sentence**, there is one *main* idea, and additional information is expressed in *subordinate* clauses. (A **clause** is a distinct part of a sentence with its own verb – see sheet 7.)

> The *girl*, **whose** dog was hurt, was unable to stop crying.

> **Main idea:** The girl was unable to stop crying.
> **Subordinate clause:** whose dog was hurt

Complex sentences should show the relationships between the ideas clearly and be interesting to read. In order to write complex sentences, you need to use *joining words*. These may be known as **conjunctions** (see sheet 5), **connectives** (see sheet 6) or **relative pronouns** (see sheet 36). Relative pronouns should always be placed as near as possible to the main subject of the sentence.

In the following examples of complex sentences, the **subject** is in *italics* and the **relative pronoun** in bold:

> *Jack*, with **whom** I had shared many good times, was unable to join us.
> The *umbrella,* under **which** we had been sheltering, blew inside out.
> There is the *fox* **that** got into the hen hut and left ten dead chickens.

Use joining words to link these sentences together to form complex sentences. You will need to change the order of the words and, in some cases, miss out or add words. (Notice the commas placed around the subordinate clause in the example.)

The boy is unable to walk quickly. He has a blister on his heel. The heel is very painful.
The boy, who has a blister on his heel, is unable to walk quickly because the heel is very painful.

1. A new girl came to school today. Her name is Maria. She is in my class.

   _____

   _____

2. The bag had been recovered. The police found it. The bag contained the missing items.

   _____

   _____

3. The shop is now closed down. I bought my first computer from it. The shop was new.

   _____

   _____

4. I am writing to thank my aunt. We stayed with her on holiday. She lives in France.

   _____

   _____

DiaGram is published by Hodder & Stoughton Educational.
The publishers grant permission for photocopies of this sheet to be made for use solely in the purchasing institution.

3

Sentences

a) All of the following begin with a capital letter and end with a full stop, but not all the groups of words are sentences. Put a tick in the first box next to the groups of words below if they form a sentence. For those you have ticked, show in the second box whether the sentence is simple (S), compound (C) or complex (X).

1. Ate two chocolates and a slice of cake. ☐ ☐

2. 'Get ready.' ☐ ☐

3. Dad said that he would wait outside until the shopping was finished. ☐ ☐

4. A crane was used to lift the heavy load. ☐ ☐

5. We put our toys away because our cousins always broke them when they came. ☐ ☐

6. Sasha, who is usually kind, gave a sweet to the child who was crying. ☐ ☐

7. Can't do his homework. ☐ ☐

8. I love painting although the results are not always very good. ☐ ☐

9. The newspaper, which often arrives at nine o'clock, came earlier today. ☐ ☐

10. It's boring. ☐ ☐

- -

b) Complete the statements using these words: verb, clause(s), equal, conjunction. Then write a short example of each type of sentence.

1. A **simple sentence** expresses one idea and contains a _____.

    Example: _____

    _____

2. A **compound sentence** contains _____.

    Example: _____

    _____

3. A **complex sentence** has more than one _____.

    Example: _____

    _____

Sentences	Secure	Work Required
Simple	☐	☐
Compound	☐	☐
Complex	☐	☐

DiaGram is published by Hodder & Stoughton Educational.
The publishers grant permission for photocopies of this sheet to be made for use solely in the purchasing institution.

Interrogatives & imperatives

The word **interrogative** is the adjective, formed from the verb *interrogate*, which means 'to question closely'. The interrogative sentence is usually asking a **question**.

Interrogative sentences may also be **statements** (e.g. *Isn't it time you were in bed?*), **instructions** (e.g. *Would you go home now, please*) and **exclamations** (e.g. *Isn't that a beautiful baby!*). Notice that if you use a question to exclaim, you use an *exclamation mark* to punctuate it, not a question mark.

Interrogative sentences are often started by an **interrogative pronoun**:

   Who?, **Whose?**, **Which?**, **What?**, To **whom**?

In addition, **interrogative adverbs** may be used. These include:

   How?, **Why?**, **Where?** and **When?** (adverb of time).

The compound words **Whatever**, **Whichever** and **Whoever** are also used to begin interrogative sentences.

What do you notice about the spelling of all but one of these 'question' words?

The words start with _____

Write five interrogative sentences.
Example: How did the chicken cross the road?

_____

_____

_____

_____

The **imperative** form of a verb is a **command**. It is direct speech and so is enclosed by speech marks – e.g. *'Stop!' 'Go!' 'Look out!'*. Often an exclamation mark is needed, because the command is also an exclamation.

An imperative verb phrase may include **do** or **don't** for emphasis – e.g. *'Do hurry.' 'Don't waste that.'*

Another form includes the contraction **let's** (short for *let us*) – e.g. *'Let's talk.'*

Imagine you are the Headteacher of your school for a day. Write on the back of this sheet some of the 'imperatives' or 'commands' you might need to say during the course of the day.
Example: 'Hurry. You'll be late for your lesson.'

DiaGram is published by Hodder & Stoughton Educational.
The publishers grant permission for photocopies of this sheet to be made for use solely in the purchasing institution.

Interrogatives & imperatives

DiaGram

Date _____

Name _____

a) **Decide the form of sentence used in the examples below. Put *In* for interrogative or *Im* for imperative in the box at the end of each sentence.**

1. 'Sit down, please,' said the coach driver. ☐
2. 'What would you like for your birthday?' ☐
3. 'When is your birthday?' ☐
4. 'Get out at once and don't come back!' shouted the angry man. ☐
5. 'Who is going to do the washing up?' ☐
6. 'You will get up at six o'clock in the morning.' ☐
7. 'Why do I have to clean my bedroom?' I said to Dad. ☐
8. 'Where are we going?' ☐
9. 'Halt. Who goes there!' ☐
10. 'Pick up that litter!' ☐

- -

b) **Explain the meaning of *interrogative*. Give an example.**

_____

_____

_____

_____

- -

c) **Explain the meaning of *imperative*. Give an example.**

_____

_____

_____

_____

Interrogatives & imperatives	Secure	Work Required
Interrogative	☐	☐
imperative	☐	☐

DiaGram is published by Hodder & Stoughton Educational.
The publishers grant permission for photocopies of this sheet to be made for use solely in the purchasing institution.

T4

Conjunctions

> **Conjunctions** (dictionary abbreviation *conj.*) are **joining words**. The most commonly used conjunctions are *and*, *but*, *because*, but many other single words can also act as conjunctions and be used to join parts of sentences together:
> I am happy **and** so are Richard and Rose.
> I am happy now **but** if you shout at me I will be sad.
> You can sit there **until** you are ready to say sorry.
> You can go out **if** you do the washing up first.

> There are two main types of conjunctions:
>
> **Coordinating conjunctions** connect words, phrases and sentences:
>
> death **or** dishonour
> He was between the devil **and** the deep blue sea.
> He got up early **but** still missed the bus.
>
> **Subordinating conjunctions** connect a simple sentence with further information:
>
> The guide was on time **although** it was an early start.

The words in the box are all joining words. The words in bold are all conjunctions.
The words in italics may also act as other parts of speech.

and	*but*	**because**	**although**	*since*	*when*	*before*	*until*	*while*
where	*after*	*neither*	*nor*	*either*	**or**	**unless**	**whether**	

Use the words from the box to complete the sentences. There are alternatives, so choose the word you prefer, first making sure that the sentences make sense.

Today is not a good day _____ it has been raining. I didn't want it to

rain _____ I had planned to work in the garden and plant out the new shrubs

I bought yesterday. I will leave them in the shed _____ I wait for the weather to improve.

Perhaps the sun will shine _____ we have had dinner. I cannot go out _____ there is

some improvement. I don't mind a spot or two of rain whilst I am working _____ a downpour

makes digging impossible. I will prepare for the worst _____ hope for the best.

> It is not usual to **start** a sentence with a conjunction – particularly *and*, *but* or *because* – although some writers do so.

DiaGram is published by Hodder & Stoughton Educational.
The publishers grant permission for photocopies of this sheet to be made for use solely in the purchasing institution.

5

Connectives

Connectives can be a word, pairs of words, or several words, used to link parts of a sentence together. The most commonly used linking words are called **conjunctions**. Examples of simple conjunctions are *and, but, that, until, if, yet*. (See sheet 5.)

Another word used to describe some words which perform this linking activity is **conjunct**. Conjuncts are used when the two groups of words being linked together could stand alone and make sense:

> I am going out now, **nevertheless** I expect you to do your homework.
> I will forgive you this time, **however** don't do it again, please.

Sometimes, pairs and groups of words such as *so that, as if, as soon as, as long as*, etc, are used to join parts of sentences together. These are called **complex conjunctions**:

> I don't mind the mess **as long as** the children are happy.

Some joining words are used in pairs: **either…or, neither…nor, not only…but also**.

- -

Use suitable connectives to link these clauses/sentences together. You will need to change some capital letters and punctuation. The first one is done for you.

The sun was burning hot. It was only ten o'clock in the morning.
<u>The sun was burning hot **even though** it was only ten o'clock in the morning.</u>

1. I like ice-cream. I prefer chips.

   _____

2. The sky was red and orange. A fire was raging.

   _____

3. We will be ready to leave. Your father returns from work.

   _____

4. I am not worried about your results. I know you have done your best.

   _____

5. I will give you your pocket money now. There will be no more later in the week.

   _____

6. They hurried to put up their umbrellas. They would not be drenched by the rain.

   _____

DiaGram is published by Hodder & Stoughton Educational.
The publishers grant permission for photocopies of this sheet to be made for use solely in the purchasing institution.

6

Conjunctions & connectives

a) Underline the *conjunctions* in these sentences.

1. I was in a hurry but I stopped to say hello.

2. We ate our supper and afterwards played on the computer.

3. I will go to the concert although the tickets are expensive.

4. The parrot ate the bird food and then proceeded to eat the flowers.

5. I would love a sports car but they can be costly both to buy and to run.

b) Join the pairs of sentences with a suitable conjunction.

1. The girls were laughing. The boys were telling jokes.

   _____

2. We went to London to see a band. We couldn't get tickets.

   _____

3. We went to the disco. We didn't stay long.

   _____

4. The train was on time. We arrived in Manchester early.

   _____

c) What job do *connectives* do in a sentence?

_____

_____

_____

d) Underline the connectives in this passage.

It was freezing cold even though it was mid-summer. Jenny and Joe wanted to go to the open air swimming pool but their parents had said no because it was too cold. 'You can either go to the park or have a friend round and they can stay for supper. Both of you have not only worked hard at school, but also been a real help at home. You deserve a treat,' said their mother.

Conjunctions & connectives	Secure	Work Required
Conjunctions	☐	☐
Connectives	☐	☐

DiaGram is published by Hodder & Stoughton Educational.
The publishers grant permission for photocopies of this sheet to be made for use solely in the purchasing institution.

T5/6

Phrases & clauses

DiaGram Date _____

Name _____

A **phrase** is a group of words which don't have their own verb and which don't make sense on their own. They **tell us more** about another word:
>The jacket **with deep pockets** was too short.

The phrase (in bold) tells us more about the jacket.

A **clause** occurs within a sentence, it contains a verb and makes sense on its own.

A **main clause** is similar to a simple sentence:
>**We went to town** and I met my friend.

A **subordinate clause** adds to the main sentence and does not stand alone:
>He stopped the man who was running away **screaming that he was hurt**.

Quite often clauses and phrases have commas around them:
>He stopped, **lifted his hand to wave**, and walked away. – *clause* (note the verb)

>The car, **a huge black sports car**, roared away into the night. – *phrase*

State whether the words in bold are a phrase or a clause by putting a 'P' or a 'C' in the brackets at the end of each line.

1.   The Taylors, **who are a noisy family**, have gone on holiday. ( )

2.   'I'm hungry, **in fact starving**,' I said when I got home from school. ( )

3.   The girls danced down the road **as if they were at a club**. ( )

4.   The teacher, **who was always loaded with things**, dropped the pile of books. ( )

5.   The words '**You're dead**' were scrawled on the postcard. ( )

6.   Meal time, **always chaotic in our house**, was at six o'clock. ( )

7.   The protesters marched **down the road**. ( )

8.   The horse **with the white blaze** came first in the race. ( )

9.   They went to the shops **because they love shopping**. ( )

10. The train, **moving slowly at first**, left the platform on time. ( )

Write two sentences of your own and underline any clauses you have included.

Example: My friend, <u>who has a terrible temper</u>, kicked the boy <u>who had called him names</u>.

_____

_____

DiaGram is published by Hodder & Stoughton Educational.
The publishers grant permission for photocopies of this sheet to be made for use solely in the purchasing institution.

7

Phrases & clauses

Date _____

Name _____

a) What is a _phrase_? _____

_____

Example: _____

- -

b) What is a _clause_? _____

_____

Example: _____

- -

c) Underline the _phrases_ in the following sentences.

1. I love to eat pancakes with sugar on Pancake Tuesday.

2. I brought my dog, a shaggy mongrel, with me today.

3. How do you use the new computer in the school library?

4. Horses, my favourite animals, are very expensive to keep.

5. The lion, with a snarl of rage, sprang at the hunter.

- -

d) Underline the _clauses_ in these sentences.

1. The houses, which were built of old stone, looked interesting.

2. Shah Jehan, who had the Taj Mahal built, did so because he loved his wife so much.

3. The Taj Mahal, which took twenty-two years to build, is a popular tourist place.

4. The boy got up and, smiling in delight, went to receive the Man of the Match award.

5. She began to sing when the conductor gave her a nod.

Phrases & clauses	Secure	Work Required
Phrase	☐	☐
Clause	☐	☐

Common nouns & articles

Nouns (dictionary abbreviation *n.*)

> A **common noun** is a **naming** word – e.g. *pencil, dog, mat, house, car, hat.*

Look at the words below and underline the common nouns, using the definition to help you:

wave   pink   snake   bed   singing   worked   left   moon   church   work
sat   bell   site   spade   before   too   talks   seat   jump   dog   flock   egg

Put common nouns into the spaces to make sense of these sentences.

1.   _____ are tasty fruits.

2.   If you eat too many _____ you will be sick.

3.   A _____ is a strong, intelligent animal.

4.   To make a _____ you will need _____ and _____.

Articles (dictionary abbreviation *art.*)

We usually use an **article** with a common noun – **the** pencil, **a** pencil; **the** dog, **a** dog.

> ### The definite article – *the*
>
> The name *definite* is helpful, because you are referring to a specific or *definite* thing when you use the article **the**:
>
> **The** window is open. We put **the** car in the garage at night.

> ### Indefinite articles – *a, an*
>
> Indefinite articles don't refer to a particular object:
> **A** window or **a** car refers to *any* window or *any* car.
>
> If a noun begins with a vowel or a silent '*h*', it is much easier to say the word if the article **a** is changed to **an**. Practise saying *a orange, an orange*; *a Indian, an Indian*.
> Can you feel how much more fluent **an** is before a vowel, in speech?

Complete these sentences with a suitable article.

1.   'Mum, please may I have _____ ice-cream?' whined Charlie.

2.   In the basket were _____ banana, _____ apple and _____ bruised plum.

3.   'Getting you lot ready on time is _____ impossible task!' said Dad.

4.   I was asked if I was _____ honest person when I applied for _____ job.

DiaGram is published by Hodder & Stoughton Educational.
The publishers grant permission for photocopies of this sheet to be made for use solely in the purchasing institution.

> **Proper nouns** are the names which make an individual different from others of its kind. They usually refer to people, places and named animals:
>
> London   Peter   English Channel   Indian Ocean   Sarah   Trigger
> Buster   Blackie   America   England
>
> **Proper** nouns are *always* written with a **capital letter** at the beginning.

Make lists of proper nouns under the headings below.

people
_____
_____
_____
_____

towns
_____
_____
_____
_____

cities
_____
_____
_____
_____

rivers
_____
_____
_____

seas
_____
_____
_____

countries
_____
_____
_____

continents
_____
_____
_____

roads
_____
_____
_____

pop stars
_____
_____
_____

films
_____
_____
_____
_____

songs
_____
_____
_____
_____

books
_____
_____
_____
_____

What is your favourite name for a...?

dog _____   cat _____   horse _____   snake _____

DiaGram is published by Hodder & Stoughton Educational.
The publishers grant permission for photocopies of this sheet to be made for use solely in the purchasing institution.

Abstract nouns

Abstract nouns are names of things we know exist but we cannot physically touch them. This group includes *feelings* and *emotions*, also *ideas*. For example:

| love | hate | kindness | art | war | work | language | hope | health | society |

Some abstract nouns can also act as other parts of speech. If the word is acting as a verb, there will be a personal pronoun (see sheet 12) or the name of a person or object before it.

Do you believe in **love** *(abstract noun)* at first sight?
I **love** *(verb)* you.

There is **hope** *(abstract noun)* that they are still alive.
We **hope** *(verb)* you are well.

Highlight or underline the abstract nouns below.

syrup	Ben	cheese	dog	calmness	plant	hope	cat	life
cart	anger	Madrid	journey	joy	Janet	mildness	patience	
holiday	heat	pencil	circus	colour	horse	hope	greed	skin
France	hunger	fish	happiness	grief	George	calm	iron	

We only write these nouns with capital letters if they come at the beginning of a sentence, if they are in a title of a film, play, book or piece of music, or if they are used as proper nouns. Joy and Patience, say, are both girls' names, as well as being abstract nouns.

Complete these well-known sayings using these abstract nouns:

| tide | work | hunger | patience | beauty | time |

1. _____ is in the eye of the beholder.

2. _____ is a virtue, possess it if you can. Seldom found in women, and never in a man!

3. _____ and _____ wait for no man.

4. Hard _____ never hurt anyone.

Write a short paragraph about yourself, using as many abstract nouns as you can. The example below may help you to get started.

I am a person who enjoys **work**. I don't like **laziness**. I have a lot of **patience** when I look after my brother and sister.

_____

_____

_____

DiaGram is published by Hodder & Stoughton Educational.
The publishers grant permission for photocopies of this sheet to be made for use solely in the purchasing institution.

10

Collective nouns

Date _____

Name _____

A **collective noun** is a singular word which groups together several of the same thing –
e.g. a **troupe** of acrobats – collective noun *troupe*. Other examples include:

pack   bunch   gang   set   class   suite   pride   herd   school   litter   fleet

Note that we use the verb in a *singular* form with a collective noun – e.g. *The litter of puppies **is**
sweet; The tribe of cannibals **has** died out; The team of athletes **was** lost.*

Choose the correct word from the examples above to complete these phrases.

1. A _____ of cows.

2. A _____ of puppies.

3. A _____ of ships.

4. A _____ of lions.

5. A _____ of furniture.

6. A _____ of thieves.

7. A _____ of spoons.

8. A _____ of wolves.

9. A _____ of children.

10. A _____ of whales.

Choose the correct collective nouns from the box to complete the sentences.

company   anthology   constellation   convoy   swarm   queue   volley

squadron   flight   congregation   brood   shoal   bouquet   choir

1. James was given an _____ of poetry for Christmas.

2. Two ships in the _____ were sunk by torpedoes.

3. The fishermen found a huge _____ of fish.

4. The _____ in the church prayed for the victims of the famine.

5. We fired a _____ of shots when the enemy broke cover.

6. The whole _____ of chicks was killed by a fox.

7. A _____ of actors came to perform at school.

8. A long _____ of people waited to buy tickets for the match.

9. The comet was first sighted in the _____ of the Great Bear.

10. All the aircraft in the _____ returned safely to base.

11. The singing of the school _____ was very good.

12. The last _____ of stairs was the steepest.

13. We were terrified when we saw the _____ of bees flying towards us.

DiaGram is published by Hodder & Stoughton Educational.
The publishers grant permission for photocopies of this sheet to be made for use solely in the purchasing institution.

Nouns

a) The code letters refer to types of nouns. Put the correct code letter in the brackets after each noun in the sentences below.

| C – common | P – proper | A – abstract | D – collective |

1. A swarm (   ) of bees (   ) was flying in the direction of the school. (   )

2. An onion (   ) is a very useful ingredient (   ) in many different types of dish.

3. 'Hatred (   ) can be a very destructive emotion (   )', said the bishop. (   )

4. Susan (   ) and Graham (   ) often go to the cinema (   ) to see the latest film. (   )

5. A dog (   ) can be an interesting and faithful friend. (   )

6. The herd (   ) was grazing peacefully in the sunshine. (   )
   _____red

7. Brian (   ) built the new wall (   ) from old bricks. (   )
   _____green

8. My favourite game (   ) is table tennis. (   ) _____orange

9. 'Please will you set the table?' (   ) Yasmin (   ) asked.

10. You should try to have patience (   ) and not lose your temper (   ) so often.

- -

b) Write three examples of each of these types of nouns.

Common: _____ _____ _____

Proper: _____ _____ _____

Abstract: _____ _____ _____

Collective: _____ _____ _____

Nouns	Secure	Work Required
Common	☐	☐
Proper	☐	☐
Abstract	☐	☐
Collective	☐	☐

T8/11

Pronouns: subject/object

It would be very difficult to keep repeating the name of something or somebody every time we wanted to refer to them. It would sound very odd. For this reason, we use other words in the place of names. We call these words **pronouns** (dictionary abbreviation *pron.*). For example:

> John plays football every day. John is good at football.
> John plays football every day. **He** is very good at **it**.

He and **it** are pronouns. They make it easier and quicker to speak or to write, and avoid repetition of the name.

The **subject** of a sentence is the *person or thing carrying out the action.*
The **object** of the sentence is *having the action done to it.*
> **I** *(subject)* will tell *(verb)* **them** *(object).*

We use the personal pronouns shown in **group 1**, below, when the name is replaced by a pronoun for the **subject** of the sentence.

Group 1: Personal pronouns (subject)

singular	plural
I	we
you	you
he/she/it	they

I run with the ball.	**We** cooked the dinner.
You will go to bed now.	**You** washed the dishes.
He/she/it is playing a game.	**They** lit the fire.

Underline the personal pronouns (subject) in these sentences.

1. 'I think these are yours,' he said.

2. 'You will like this ice-cream. I made it myself.'

3. 'I will take one of each type, please.'

We use the personal pronouns shown in **group 2**, below, when the name is replaced by a pronoun for the **object** of the sentence.

Group 2: Personal pronouns (object)

singular	plural
me	us
you	you
him/her/it	them

Give the ball to **me**.	Let him pay **us**.
Let James go with **you**.	They will come to **you** both.
Don't let Jo tease **him/her/it**.	Rashid gave it to **them**.

Underline the personal pronouns (object) in the following sentences.

1. My dog enjoys her bones. She likes them.

2. Will you please let me have the chocolate now?

3. They liked to play with them because they were fun.

DiaGram is published by Hodder & Stoughton Educational.
The publishers grant permission for photocopies of this sheet to be made for use solely in the purchasing institution.

Types of pronouns

The pronouns in groups 3 to 7, below, have different jobs to do in sentences. The name of each group tells you something about the job.

Group 3: Possessive pronouns show who owns or possesses something or someone:

singular	*plural*
mine	ours
yours	yours
his/hers/its	theirs

For example: You can't take that, it's **mine**.

Fill in the missing possessive pronoun.

1. Shall we take my car or _____?   *2.* Well, have this desk, you can share _____ .

Group 4: Reflexive pronouns reflect back to an earlier noun or pronoun:

singular	*plural*
myself	ourselves
yourself	yourselves
himself, herself, itself	themselves

For example: They did it **themselves**.

Underline or highlight the reflexive pronoun AND the name or pronoun it is relating to, as shown in the example.

Example: Can **you** do it **yourself**?

1. Simon can please himself, but I would like to go.   *2.* Jo ate a whole chocolate cake herself.

Group 5: Interrogative pronouns – e.g. *who?, whose?, whom?, which?, what?* – interrogate or ask questions.

For example: **Who** did this?

Complete these sentences with an interrogative pronoun.

1. _____ time is it?   *2.* To _____ does this belong?

Group 6: Demonstrative pronouns – e.g. *this, that, these, those* – point out or demonstrate a person or thing specifically.

For example: **This** is the one I want. I don't like **that** one. I'll take six of **them**.

Group 7: Indefinite pronouns refer to people or things *generally* rather than specifically. They are *not* definite – e.g. *any, each, several, some*.

For example: Do you want **any** breakfast? **Some** of **each**, please.

DiaGram is published by Hodder & Stoughton Educational.
The publishers grant permission for photocopies of this sheet to be made for use solely in the purchasing institution.

13

Pronouns

a) Give two examples of each of the following types of pronouns:

1. **personal pronouns: subject:** _____ _____

2. **personal pronouns: object:** _____ _____

3. **possessive pronouns:** _____ _____

4. **reflexive pronouns:** _____ _____

5. **interrogative pronouns:** _____ _____

6. **demonstrative pronouns:** _____ _____

7. **indefinite pronouns:** _____ _____

---

b) Use pronouns instead of the proper nouns shown in bold in the passage. Write them in the spaces provided after the names. The letters in italics change when the proper nouns are changed to pronouns. The first two are done for you.

Surjit was cross with Martin. [**Surjit**] _____He_____ said to Martin, 'I hate [**Martin**] _____you_____ .'

Martin said to Surjit, '[**Martin**] _____ hate(*s*) [**Surjit**] _____ too. What can [**Surjit**]

_____ do about it, then?'

'[**Surjit**] _____ will hit [**Martin**] _____ very hard if [**Martin**] _____ doesn't (*don't*) stop

taking [**Surjit's**] _____ pen and scribbling on [**Surjit's**] _____ work.'

'That pen is not [**Surjit's**] _____ pen, it is [**Martin's**] _____ .'

'It is not [**Martin's**] _____ pen. It is [**Surjit's**] _____ pen.'

A teacher came across to see what the shouting was about.

'I don't know whether it is [**Martin's**] _____ pen, Martin or [**Surjit's**] _____ pen, Surjit. Right now

it is [**Teacher's**] _____ pen, because [**Teacher**] _____ will keep it until the end of the lesson.'

Pronouns	Secure	Work Required
Pronouns	☐	☐

DiaGram is published by Hodder & Stoughton Educational.
The publishers grant permission for photocopies of this sheet to be made for use solely in the purchasing institution.

Singular & plural

When we use the word **singular** (dictionary abbreviation *sing.*), we mean **one** thing.

When we use the word **plural** (dictionary abbreviation *pl.*), we mean **more than one** thing.

This doesn't just affect the spelling of the **nouns** – we also have to change some **pronouns**, **verbs** and **demonstrative adjectives**.

It is useful to look at **pronouns** and how they change in singular and plural. It is important to understand their purpose, not only for use in English, but also for when you learn another language. It is helpful to see the pattern of changing words and word endings from person to person and from singular to plural:

	singular	*plural*
1st person	I	we
2nd person	you	you
3rd person	he/she/it	they

It is usually the third person singular form of the **verb** which changes. We usually add an '**-s**' to the verb: *they run* but *he run**s**, they walk – she walk**s**, they eat – it eat**s**.*
Some verbs don't follow this pattern and the words change completely in the plural. We call them **irregular** verbs. Examples are: *I **was**/ we **were**, it **has**/ they **have**.*

Demonstrative adjectives are linked to nouns, and change from singular to plural:

I would like **this** book. I have already read **those** books.
I will take **that** jacket, at **these** prices it is a bargain.

Changes to the spelling of **nouns** from singular to plural vary – e.g. *bag/ bags* and *dress/ dresses*, but *child/ children, mouse/ mice*, etc. (Note also that the indefinite article *'a'* or *'an'* can change to *'some'*.)

Change these sentences from singular to plural.
Think about which words need to be altered.

1. The dog wanted his dinner.

   _____

2. The child had a pet mouse.

   _____

3. I went to the shop to buy a loaf of bread.

   _____

4. The baby was crying for his mother.

   _____

DiaGram is published by Hodder & Stoughton Educational.
The publishers grant permission for photocopies of this sheet to be made for use solely in the purchasing institution.

14

Singular & plural

Date _____

Name _____

a) Change the words in these sentences which are followed by brackets, from singular to plural. Write the new word within the brackets. Words in bold are missed out in the plural. Remember, it is not just nouns which change.

1. The computer (_____) was (_____) loaded with **a** game

   (_____) which looked very interesting.

2. The child (_____) shouted with excitement when he (_____) saw the

   monkey (_____) in the tree (_____).

3. The man (_____) struggled to keep hold of his (_____)

   umbrella (_____) in the high wind (_____).

4. She (_____) went to **a** different country (_____) every year for

   her (_____) holiday (_____).

5. I (_____) like to eat **a** sweet (_____) or **some** chocolate

   (_____) for a treat.

6. **A** thief (_____) broke into the house (_____) and stole **a** television

   (_____) and **a** video (_____).

7. **A** mouse (_____) was (_____) running about the house. (_____).

8. The painting (_____) was (_____) the work of **a** famous

   artist (_____).

- -

b) Write the plurals of the words below.

   1. mouse _____   2. house _____   3. die _____

   4. salmon _____   5. child _____   6. ox _____

Singular & plural	Secure	Work Required
Singular/plural	☐	☐

DiaGram is published by Hodder & Stoughton Educational.
The publishers grant permission for photocopies of this sheet to be made for use solely in the purchasing institution.

T14

Adjectives – describing

Adjectives (dictionary abbreviation *adj.*) tell us **more about** things or people. We use adjectives to make descriptions lively and interesting. The descriptions can be spoken or written. You need to choose adjectives carefully, so that they say exactly what you mean.

If you use two or more adjectives to describe one noun, it can be very effective if each adjective starts with the same letter – this is called **alliteration** (see sheet 54):

great, **g**reedy cat;   **v**icious, **v**indictive **v**iper;   **b**eautiful, **b**ubbly girl.

Be careful that you don't use *too* many adjectives and that you don't repeat the same ones too often, or they will then lose their effectiveness.
Nice, great, lovely, boring are often over-used words. Try to think of other words which will create the same 'word picture':

Nice: pleasant, splendid, wonderful, super, terrific.
Boring: uninteresting, flat, unimaginative, repetitive.

Note that **colours** and **numbers** are adjectives.

You need to work hard to build up a store of adjectives. Use a thesaurus or a dictionary. Listen to other people talking. Read carefully and make a note of words you think are effective in describing people, places, things or emotions.

Some words can be changed so that they become adjectives:

Zoo is a noun, but becomes an adjective in the phrase *zoo cats*.

Verbs can also be used as adjectives. *To watch* is a verb, but *watchful* is an adjective:
The watchful hound saw his master pick up the dog lead.

Choose an animal, a person, a thing or a place and make an A–Z of adjectives to describe your choice.
Examples: An **a**ngry dog, **b**atty hound, **c**urly-tailed cur, **d**opey dog, **e**ager dog, etc.

Highlight or underline the adjectives in the passage below.

It was a horrible evening. Billowing clouds heralded yet another downpour of stinging, freezing rain which would make even the most adventurous walker quail at the thought of the long weary miles ahead. Each person was carrying emergency rations, water, extra warm, waterproof clothing, a compass, flashlight and a map. Nobody knew for certain what conditions would be like on the bleak moors at this time of year. Thorough preparation was essential if the three missing children were to be successfully located and returned safely to their frantic parents. A day of bright sunshine and blue skies had been transformed into a frightening world where it was difficult to see a step in front of you because of the blinding rain. The children had set off on a short ramble up the steep, stone strewn hillside. That was eight hours ago. What had happened to them?

DiaGram is published by Hodder & Stoughton Educational.
The publishers grant permission for photocopies of this sheet to be made for use solely in the purchasing institution.

Adjectives – comparing

We use different endings to **compare** qualities which describe something or someone, depending upon whether two or more than two people or things are involved. The terms we use are **comparative** (for *two*) and **superlative** (for *more than two*). The *comparative* ending is -**er**. The *superlative* ending is -**est**.

> 'I am clever**er** than you.' – *comparative adjective*
> 'No, you're not. I'm the clever**est** person in the class.' – *superlative adjective*

Write the two forms of these adjectives under the headings as in the example.

Adjective	Comparative	Superlative
fat	fatter	fattest
1. tall	_____	_____
2. high	_____	_____
3. small	_____	_____

Read this carefully!

If a word is long and would be difficult to pronounce with a suffix -**er** or -**est**, you say **more** for two people or things (*comparative*), **most** for more than two (*superlative*):

> The girl was *more graceful* than her sister, in fact the *most graceful* skater we had ever seen. Her brother was the *most handsome* boy in the show.

Not every word obeys the rules. We can say *louder* or *more loudly*, *loudest* or *most loud*. You have to learn the exceptions to the rules.

Use these words to form sentences of your own.

beautiful   handsome   irritating

_____

_____

_____

_____

Complete these sentences using the correct form of the adjectives *good* and *bad*.

1. This is the _____ day I've ever spent. *(bad)*

2. Can't you do _____ than that? *(good)*

3. The weather may get _____ *(bad)*, before it gets _____. *(good)*

DiaGram is published by Hodder & Stoughton Educational.
The publishers grant permission for photocopies of this sheet to be made for use solely in the purchasing institution.

16

Adjectives – possession

> These words show **ownership** and so we call them **possessive adjectives**:
> my   his   her   its   our   your   their

> Be careful when you use the possessive pronoun **its** – e.g. *The cat ate its fish quickly.*
> Don't confuse **its** with the contraction **it's**, which is short for *it is* or *it has.*
> Say your sentence aloud and decide whether you are trying to say *it is* or *it has.*
> If you are not, *don't* use an apostrophe.

Underline the possessive adjectives in this passage. Insert apostrophes of omission (e.g. *it's* when it means *it is*) where they are needed.

1. 'You cant use this computer, its mine,' shouted Gail at her brother.

2. 'It isnt fair,' he replied.

3. 'Thats true', interjected their mother. 'You always borrowed his before you had one of your own.'

4. 'Well', Gail said, realising the truth of this statement. 'He can use his own now all the time and only use mine when Im out, if he wants the latest technology.'

5. 'If you two dont stop arguing, Ill give them both to the school. I hear that most of theirs are broken,' mother answered.

6. 'Oh! Please dont do that. Well use ours sensibly from now on. Honestly,' both children called out. They were together for once in their thinking.

- -

Complete these sentences with an appropriate possessive adjective. Add any punctuation you think is necessary.

1. My big brother is taller than _____ big brother.

2. 'I've been giving _____ roses a feed today,' said George.
   'Why, were they hungry?' asked Fred.

3. My dog will never eat _____ biscuits.

4. Don't blame me, its _____ fault.

5. The watch needs _____ face replacing. Its scratched.

6. I hope you are not going to throw one of _____ tantrums.

7. The boys returned to _____ school with the football trophy.

8. When we say _____ house, we mean the house in which we live.

9. The girl showed us _____ engagement ring with pride.

10. The boy wore _____ new trainers to go to the gym.

DiaGram is published by Hodder & Stoughton Educational.
The publishers grant permission for photocopies of this sheet to be made for use solely in the purchasing institution.

17

Adjectives

DiaGram
Date _____
Name _____

a) Underline or highlight the adjectives in the passage.

We arrived at the popular beach about two o'clock in the afternoon. The sizzling sun made us move quickly to the welcome shade of a bright blue sun-umbrella. We looked around. Beautiful tanned girls and boys were lying on white sun-beds listening to the loud pop music which came from the huge speakers at the beach bar. Every few minutes, they stroked sun-tan lotion into their bronzed skin to protect themselves from the harmful rays of the burning sun. Laughing children swam in the shallow, turquoise sea, supervised by anxious grandparents. It was a holiday beach devoted to the pursuit of pure pleasure.

b) Complete these sentences by using the correct comparative or superlative form of the adjective in brackets at the end of each line.

1. The elder Jones' boy is _____ than his brother. *(tall)*

2. Natasha is the _____ runner in the school. *(fast)*

3. My writing is _____ than yours. *(bad)*

4. Do you think I am _____ than my sister? *(beautiful)*

5. I find division sums the _____ of all. *(difficult)*

c) Underline the possessive adjectives in the passage.

Most people like to have their own things – and so do I. The trouble is, my younger brothers and sisters think that everything which is mine, should be theirs. My mother says that you should share your things. I agree with her. I do share my books and toys, but they don't. Even the dog has its own belongings which he keeps to himself. Our house seems to be filled with people arguing about whether it's *his* play station or *her* pen. Of course I'm the one who has to give in, because I'm the oldest. One day I'll have my own room and in it everything will be mine; nobody will be allowed in, not even my parents.

Adjectives	Secure	Work Required
Describing	☐	☐
Comparative	☐	☐
Possessive	☐	☐

DiaGram is published by Hodder & Stoughton Educational.
The publishers grant permission for photocopies of this sheet to be made for use solely in the purchasing institution.

Finite & non-finite verbs

> **Verbs** (dictionary abbreviation *v.*) are words or groups of words which show an *action* or a *state of being*.
>
> **Finite verbs** form a *tense* and have a *subject*:
>   **He** (*subject*) **is singing** *(verb, present tense)* at the top of his voice.

Read the following sentences.
Write the subject and the finite verb in the spaces provided.

1. James fell off his motorbike.   *Subject* _____ *Finite verb* _____

2. The aeroplane flew over the mountains.   *Subject* _____ *Finite verb* _____

3. The ship sank to the bottom of the sea.   *Subject* _____ *Finite verb* _____

4. The gardener mowed the lawns before the rain. *Subject* _____ *Finite verb* _____

> **Agreement of subject and verb**. Every finite verb has a subject, which may be singular or plural. **The verb and subject must agree**. If the *subject* is *singular*, the *verb* must be *singular*; if the *subject* is *plural*, the *verb* must be *plural*, whatever the tense:
>
>   **I am** singing / **they are** singing   **I was** singing / **we were** singing

> Some parts of the verb do not form tenses. They are called **non-finite.**
>
> - The **infinitive** is the root of the verb and usually has the word **to** in front – e.g. **to** *laugh*, **to** *dance*.
> - The **present participle** usually ends in **-ing** – e.g. *cook**ing**, fight**ing**, play**ing**.*
> - The **past participle** usually ends in **-ed**. Irregular forms end in **-d**, **-t**, or **-en** – e.g. *jump**ed**, fough**t**, bitt**en**.*
>
> The present and past participles are used with **auxiliary verbs** (see sheet 20):
>
>   I am crying.   They are shouting.   He was bitten.

Underline the infinitive verbs in these sentences.

1. To walk to the shops will be good exercise.
2. Playing out in the fresh air is good for you.
3. Sleeping is my favourite occupation.
4. To fight is not usually a good way to solve a problem.
5. It was forbidden to play on the grass.
6. Playing a musical instrument is very hard.
7. To swing from the trees is fun.
8. Eating hay in a field all day seems a very boring way to live.

DiaGram is published by Hodder & Stoughton Educational.
The publishers grant permission for photocopies of this sheet to be made for use solely in the purchasing institution.

18

Verb – participles

Participles are parts of a verb. They are called participles because they 'participate', or take part, in forming the verb. They usually follow the auxiliary verb *to be* and *to have*. (See sheet 20 to learn more about auxiliary verbs.)

> The **present participle** is the part of the verb which ends in **-ing**. It is used with the auxiliary verb to form all tenses in the continuous form of the verb. This means that the action *continues to happen*. It is not a completed action:
>
> I am walking.   We are laughing.   They are crying.

> The **past participle** is the part of the verb we use when the action *has already taken place*.
> It usually follows **has**, **have**, **had** or **was**.
> It usually ends in **-ed**, but some words are irregular: they may end in **-d**, **-t**, **-en**, **-n** – or change completely, as in *fight/fought*, *bite/bitten*:
>
> She had walked.   They have fought.   He has bitten.

> *Note:* **Past** is to do with *time* when we use it to talk about verbs. The word **passed**, which sounds the same, means to overtake something (e.g. *The car* **passed** *the bus*) or to be successful (e.g. *I have* **passed** *my music exam*).

- -

Write down the present and past participles of the verbs shown below in the spaces provided.

	Verb	Present participle	Past participle
1.	run	_____	_____
2.	play	_____	_____
3.	jump	_____	_____
4.	fight	_____	_____
5.	kill	_____	_____
6.	knit	_____	_____
7.	speak	_____	_____
8.	grow	_____	_____
9.	fly	_____	_____

> The **gerund** also has the same **-ing** ending as the present participle, but can be used as a noun or a verb: **Staring** at people is rude. (*noun*)   You are **staring** at me. (*verb*)

DiaGram is published by Hodder & Stoughton Educational.
The publishers grant permission for photocopies of this sheet to be made for use solely in the purchasing institution.

19

The main **auxiliary verbs** are *to be* and *to have*.
The **pronouns** (words which *take the place* of names) are highlighted in the chart below.

To be

Present tense

I am	**we** are
you are	**you** are
he/she/it is	**they** are

Past tense

I was	**we** were
you were	**you** were
he/she/it was	**they** were

To have

Present tense

I have	**we** have
you have	**you** have
he/she/it has	**they** have

Past tense

I had	**we** had
you had	**you** had
he/she/it had	**they** had

Auxiliary verbs are used to help other verbs say exactly what we want them to say. They help, with a noun or pronoun and a main verb, to form the tenses. When people talk about the **person** when discussing verbs, they mean *who* or *what* is doing the action. The word we use before the verb or parts of a verb to indicate the person is a **noun** or **pronoun**. Examples of the use of auxiliary verbs are: **He is** *talking*. **They have** *worked*.

Have can be used as a main *and* as an auxiliary verb – e.g. **I have had** *my holiday.*

Additional auxiliaries are needed to form parts of the verb which express **mood**. They are not main verbs, but help us to say exactly what we mean: *We should…, you shall…, we might…, we ought to…, he used to…, she could…, they can…, I may…, we will…, they would…, we used to…*

The verb *to do* is used to form negatives and ask questions (see sheet 21).

- -

Highlight the auxiliary verbs in these sentences.

1. I will be playing football in the first team on Saturday.

2. We ought to do the tidying up today.

3. We shall be going to the cinema next week.

4. We could see the game from the kitchen window.

5. I can run as fast as the wind.

6. I am coming to the concert with you.

7. We have been very busy this term.

8. He may be late because he was kept in for being cheeky.

9. I am going to finish this, if it's the last thing I do.

10. They couldn't sing to save their lives.

DiaGram is published by Hodder & Stoughton Educational.
The publishers grant permission for photocopies of this sheet to be made for use solely in the purchasing institution.

20

Auxiliary verbs – *to do*

doesn't   did   done   does   do   don't

In order to ask questions (**interrogatives**) and to make **negatives** (denying or refusing something), we need to use the verb **to do**:

Do you come here often?   I **don't** like eating meat.

Note the different form (*does*, *doesn't*) in the third person singular:

Present tense		*Past tense*	
I do	we do	I did	we did
you do	you do	you did	you did
he/she/it does	they do	he/she/it did	they did

Negative present tense		*Negative past tense*	
I don't	we don't	I didn't	we didn't
you don't	you don't	you didn't	you didn't
he/she/it doesn't	they don't	he/she/it didn't	they didn't

**Use a form of the verb *to do* to complete each of these sentences.
The spelling will need to change depending on the person (*who* is doing it) and the tense (*when* it is being done).**

1. John wants to go to the match and so _____ Jane.

2. What _____ he mean when he says that he _____ want to go?

3. That poor man _____ look strong enough to carry on working _____ he?

4. Jenny will _____ the talking, she always _____ .

5. '_____ you always work as hard as this?' he was asked.

6. '_____ make the same mistake again,' the boss said.

7. 'If you have _____ your best it is good enough for me,' said Dad.

8. 'It _____ _____ to show off,' my mother said.

9. 'Why have you _____ that?'

10. 'When _____ you get your games console?'

Write sentences of your own using the verb *to do* in any form shown above.

_____

_____

_____

_____

DiaGram is published by Hodder & Stoughton Educational.
The publishers grant permission for photocopies of this sheet to be made for use solely in the purchasing institution.

21

Auxiliary verbs

a) Underline the auxiliary verbs in these sentences.

1. I am happy today.

2. You are lucky to have such a nice Mum and Dad.

3. We have worked hard today.

4. They were late for school yesterday.

5. You are cooking dinner for us on Saturday.

6. We had to get ready quickly.

7. They were trying to rescue the swimmer.

8. We might catch the bus if we hurry.

9. He ought to try harder.

10. We should laugh more often.

b) Fill in the missing words in these sentences using the verb *to do*.

1. '_____ you like ice-cream?'

2. '_____ your cat sleep on your bed?'

3. He _____ like getting up in the morning.

4. '_____ go out until you've cleaned your teeth.'

5. She _____ do very much work.

6. They have _____ as much as they can.

7. '_____ you sleep well last night?'

8. 'I _____ see you at the party.'

9. We _____ _____ _____ press-ups today.

10. It _____ _____ to be boastful.

c) Write five sentences using other auxiliary verbs.

_____

_____

_____

_____

_____

Auxiliary verbs	Secure	Work Required
Auxiliary verbs	☐	☐

DiaGram is published by Hodder & Stoughton Educational.
The publishers grant permission for photocopies of this sheet to be made for use solely in the purchasing institution.

Verbs – active & passive voices

> Dad cooked the dinner.   The dinner was cooked by dad.
>
> In both examples, the dinner is cooked, but the way the verb is written changes the *way* in which the action takes place. These two ways of writing the verb are known as **active** and **passive**

The active voice:
Mike played his guitar. Mike is doing the action of playing. He is **active**.

The passive voice:
The guitar was played by Mike. In this sentence, the guitar is having the action *done to it*. The guitar is **passive**.

> The **active** voice is used more often than the passive, because it is more direct and easier to say. It can sometimes sound a bit *too* direct. If you want to sound more polite when writing out a notice or order, the passive sounds less bossy.
>
> **Active:**   KEEP YOUR DOG ON A LEAD.
>
> **Passive:**   DOGS MUST BE KEPT ON A LEAD.

Change these sentences so that the verbs are in the passive voice. The first one is done for you.

The dog chewed the bone.
<u>The bone was chewed by the dog.</u>

1.   The cat ate the huge black spider.

_____

2.   Rosa cleans the car every week.

_____

3.   The burglars hid the money under the bed.

_____

4.   Julian threw the rubbish into the bin.

_____

- -

Change this notice from active to passive.   *CLOSE THE DOOR*

_____

DiaGram is published by Hodder & Stoughton Educational.
The publishers grant permission for photocopies of this sheet to be made for use solely in the purchasing institution.

22

Verbs – active & passive voices

a) Show whether the verb in each sentence is used in the active or the passive voice by writing 'A' or 'P' in the brackets after each verb.

1. The garden was dug (   ) by a local gardener.

2. I always dig (   ) the garden myself.

3. They fed (   ) the dog raw meat.

4. The cover had been made (   ) by hand.

5. The book had been read (   ) many times.

- -

b) Change these sentences from the passive to the active voice.

1. The keyboard was played by a very good musician.

    _____

2. The lesson was taught by a supply teacher.

    _____

3. The kite was flown by a boy and his sister.

    _____

4. The omelet was made by the cook.

    _____

5. The plane was flown by the pilot.

    _____

- -

c) Change these sentences from the active to the passive voice.

1. Peter makes his bed.

    _____

2. The ghost frightened the family.

    _____

3. Jane wrote the letter.

    _____

4. Mum picked some strawberries.

    _____

5. Dad mended the car.

    _____

Verbs	Secure	Work Required
Active/passive	☐	☐

DiaGram is published by Hodder & Stoughton Educational.
The publishers grant permission for photocopies of this sheet to be made for use solely in the purchasing institution.

Verbs – tenses

I shout   I shouted   I will shout   shouting   to shout

Verbs are _doing_ or _being_ words. They help us talk about **when** things happen and whether things are done **once** or **continue** for some time. The examples above are just a few of the ways in which we use verbs to say when and how things are done.

Present tense:	I shout / I am shouting the answer.	_It is happening now._
Past tense:	I shouted the answer.	_It has happened._
Future tense:	I will shout the answer.	_It will happen._

The **infinitive** form of the verb tells us about an action without saying _when_ it happens.
The verbs _to eat, to sing, to scream_, etc, are all doing words, but we don't know _when_, or for _how long_, the action takes place (see sheet 18).

The **present and past participles** of verbs such as _painting, running_, etc, are used to make tenses of verbs, but on their own, they don't have tense or time (see sheet 19).
For example: 'I like **painting** _(present participle)_' does not tell us _when_ the painting will take place or _how long_ it will last.

Important! Every finite verb (see sheet 18) has a subject, which may be singular or plural.
The verb and subject must agree. If the _subject_ is _singular_, the _verb_ must be _singular_;
if the _subject_ is _plural_, the _verb_ must be _plural_, whatever the tense:

I am singing / **they are** singing   **I was** singing / **we were** singing

Highlight the verbs in the passage.

I have a friend coming round for a sleep-over tonight. I don't know what time we'll get to sleep. The last time I had a friend to sleep here, my mother said it would be the last because we talked and talked half the night, keeping everyone awake. I promised Mum that this time we would be good. 'To promise is one thing. To keep the promise is another, with you.' She sighed.

Poor Mum! She works so hard and is often alone because Dad's job is far away and he doesn't get home until bedtime. That is why she is giving me this treat. I will be good and I'll make my friend behave as well. We will go to bed when we are asked. We'll not put the TV on loud, we'll not put biscuit crumbs in the bed or have the dog upstairs.

Oh dear! If we are going to be that good, it hardly seems worth asking someone round.

- -

Now write some of the highlighted verbs under the correct heading.

Present	_Past_	_Future_
_____	_____	_____
_____	_____	_____
_____	_____	_____
_____	_____	_____

DiaGram is published by Hodder & Stoughton Educational.
The publishers grant permission for photocopies of this sheet to be made for use solely in the purchasing institution.

23

Verbs – present tense

Date _____

Name _____

I drive   you sing   he laughs   she cries   it eats   we fall   you shriek   they drink

Verbs are used to help us talk about *when* things happen. If things are happening 'now', we say they are in the **present tense**. Notice that when you use the third person singular (*he/she/it*), an '**-s**' is added. The present tense can be divided into the **present simple** and the **present continuous** tenses.

Present simple

A noun or pronoun is added to the verb to tell us that a completed action is taking place now – e.g. **I ride** *my bike.* **He rides** *his bike.* **They ride** *their bikes.*

Write five sentences using different verbs in the present simple tense.
Example: I eat my breakfast at seven o'clock.

_____

_____

_____

_____

_____

Present continuous

The **present continuous** form of the verb shows that something is *happening over time* – e.g. **I am riding** *my bike.* The tense is formed by using the verb **to be** and the **present participle**. Remember the present participle ends in **-ing**.

Write the present continuous tense of the words below in the first person singular, third person singular and first person plural. The first is done for you.

1st person singular (I)	*3rd person singular (he/she/it)*	*1st person plural (we)*
laugh: I am laughing	He is laughing	We are laughing
1. cry _____	_____	_____
2. jump _____	_____	_____
3. sing _____	_____	_____
4. dance _____	_____	_____

Verbs – present perfect &
perfect continuous

Present perfect tense

The **present perfect** tense is formed by using the *present simple* (see sheet 24) of the verb **to have** (*have/has*) and the **past participle** (see sheet 19) of the main verb – e.g. **I have cleaned** *my bike*. Remember that the past participle of a verb usually ends in **-ed**.

> **I have laughed** many times at the same joke.
> **You have painted** that view often.
> **He has looked** like that before.
> **We have walked** down that road all our lives.
> **You have talked** to them at all the parties.
> **They have skated** on the pond whenever it has been frozen.

Choose any verb and write it out in the present perfect tense.

I _____   we _____

you _____   you _____

he/she/it _____   they _____

Present perfect continuous tense

The **present perfect continuous** tense also needs an *auxiliary* verb (see sheet 20) to form the tense. The present simple of the verb **to have** (*have* or *has*) is used with the **past participle** of the verb **to be** (*been*) and the **present participle** of the main verb (ends in **-ing**) – e.g. **I have been riding** *my bike*.

> **I have been writing** a letter to my gran since last month.
> **You have been sleeping** very well recently.
> **It has been swimming** around the goldfish bowl all day.
> **We have been running** six miles every day.
> **You have been preparing** the food for the party for a week.

Underline the verbs in the following passage which are in the present perfect continuous tense.

'You have been playing truant again,' said Dad in a furious voice.

'I have not,' Michael replied indignantly. 'I have been training for the school Marathon.'

'I saw you down by the river. You have been getting low grades this term and now I know why: you don't attend the lessons,' Dad yelled. All his attempts to keep calm had flown out of the window.

'I have been running, with the permission of my teachers, to give the school a chance of winning the cup on Saturday,' Michael said with dignity. 'You have been imagining the worst because you just don't trust me. Thank goodness my teachers do.'

Verbs – past tense

Past simple tense

We use the **past simple** tense when actions have happened in the *past* and for a *short time*. The action is *completed*. The ending of this form of the verb is usually -**ed**, but there are *irregular* forms of the verbs which need to be learned (see sheets 27 and 28).

I played   I jumped   I shouted   I ran *(irregular)*   I ate *(irregular)*

Change these sentences from the present to the past tense.

1. I laugh at my brother's jokes.

   _____

2. We climb the hill to go to the castle.

   _____

3. Kate jumps up and down in her excitement.

   _____

4. Philip works hard at his homework.

   _____

5. I drop my towel on the bathroom floor.

   _____

6. We cook our sausages on the barbecue.

   _____

7. We play in the school orchestra.

   _____

Past continuous tense

We use the **past continuous** tense when the action or state of being *continues* for a period of time at some time in the *past*. – e.g. **I was riding** *my bike.*

The **past continuous** is formed by using the **past simple** of the verb **to be** (*was/were*) and the **present participle** (see sheet 19) of the main verb.

I was cooking.   We were dancing.   They were writing.

Underline the verbs in the past continuous in these sentences.

1. I was going to write but I ran out of time.
2. The kettle was boiling but it has switched itself off.
3. The kite was flying high and then the wind dropped.
4. A dog was walking down the road sniffing at the telegraph posts.
5. A man was digging the garden furiously.

DiaGram is published by Hodder & Stoughton Educational.
The publishers grant permission for photocopies of this sheet to be made for use solely in the purchasing institution.

Verbs – irregular past simple 1

> Usually, main verbs in the **past tense** end in -**ed.** Sometimes, however, verbs change completely in the past tense. You have to learn these exceptions.
>
> Verbs which *don't* end in -**ed** in the past simple tense have an ***irregular*** **past simple** tense – for example:
>
> ate   took   drank   lied   taught   grew   told

Complete the sentences using the past simple tense. Read each sentence aloud. The first one is done for you.

Present	Past
I **see**	I **saw** a cat catching a rat.

1. He **finds**   He **found** _____
2. You **steal**   You **stole** _____
3. I **tread**   I **trod** _____
4. I **catch**   I **caught** _____
5. They **ride**   They **rode** _____
6. We **take**   We **took** _____
7. I **blow**   I **blew** _____
8. I **draw**   I **drew** _____
9. We **hold**   We **held** _____
10. He **fights**   He **fought** _____
11. I **write**   I **wrote** _____
12. I **buy**   I **bought** _____

- -

Write sentences of your own containing these words.
Example: bought – I bought myself an ice-cream.

1. blew _____
2. brought _____
3. flew _____
4. drew _____

DiaGram is published by Hodder & Stoughton Educational.
The publishers grant permission for photocopies of this sheet to be made for use solely in the purchasing institution.

Verbs – irregular past simple 2

DiaGram

Date _____

Name _____

| was | had | spoke | paid | sang | gave | flew | swam | sold | lit | hung | read |

Look at the words in the box, then write the simple past tense of the following words. Have your work checked before you continue.

1. light _____

2. fly _____

3. sell _____

4. read _____

5. pay _____

6. am _____

7. swim _____

8. speak _____

9. have _____

10. give _____

11. hang _____

12. sing _____

- -

Change the word in brackets at the end of each sentence so that it is in the past tense. Write it in the space provided in the sentence. The first one is done for you.

Last year I <u>went</u> to London three times. *(go)*

1. Mr Smith _____ me Maths last year. *(teach)*

2. He _____ off the wall but didn't hurt himself. *(fall)*

3. It _____ to rain an hour ago. *(begin)*

4. He _____ it so well that we can't find it. *(hide)*

5. The boys _____ waiting for the Headmaster to punish them. *(stand)*

6. Where _____ you hide my pen? *(do)*

7. It was so cold last week the pond _____. *(freeze)*

8. I _____ my trainers to the match. *(wear)*

9. Where _____ you put the newspaper? *(do)*

10. The cat _____ on the mat feeling very bored. *(sit)*

11. I was in terrible trouble when I _____ the glass dish. *(break)*

12. They _____ vegetables in their garden. *(grow)*

13. The lady _____ her washing out every day. *(hangs)*

14. They _____ everything very cheaply in the market. *(sell)*

15. I _____ tired because of working on the computer for too long. *(am)*

DiaGram is published by Hodder & Stoughton Educational.
The publishers grant permission for photocopies of this sheet to be made for use solely in the purchasing institution.

Verbs – past perfect & past perfect continuous

Past perfect tense

> We form the **past perfect** tense by using the **past simple** of the verb **to have** (*had*), with the **past participle** of the main verb (e.g. *walked, climbed*):
>
> I **had** *walked*   they **had** *climbed*.

Change the verbs in these sentences into the past perfect tense. Add more words to the sentence to make it more interesting. The first is done for you as an example. Notice that when you use the past perfect tense, it is easy to add on words so that the sentence tells you more.

I **watched** too much television. *(past simple)*
I **had watched** too much television and my eyes were tired. *(past perfect)*

1. We **jumped** the stream easily.

   _____

2. We **played** in a local cricket match.

   _____

3. Sarah **rode** all day.

   _____

4. They **skimmed** stones across lake.

   _____

5. She **floated** on her back in the pool.

   _____

Past perfect continuous tense

> **I had been playing** in the team, but now I wanted to join a different one.
>
> The **past perfect continuous** is formed by using the **past simple** of the verb **to have** (*had*), with the **past participle** of the verb **to be** (*been*), and the **present participle** of the main verb (ending in -**ing**) – e.g. *I* **had been crying**, *we* **had been playing**, etc.

Underline the verbs in the past perfect continuous tense in these sentences.

1. I had been going to go for a walk, but I was too lazy.
2. The potatoes had been boiling so I turned them down to a simmer.
3. The aircraft had been flying very low before it crashed.
4. The man had been walking his dog in the woods when he found the body.
5. The woman had been going to offer a reward.
6. The boy had been running towards the road before we heard the scream.
7. We had been promising to take the twins out.

DiaGram is published by Hodder & Stoughton Educational.
The publishers grant permission for photocopies of this sheet to be made for use solely in the purchasing institution.

The future is something which has not happened yet, but we still talk, read and write about it – e.g. *Next year we will go to Spain in June.*

Future simple tense

> The **future simple** tense is formed by using **will** or **shall** before the main verb:
>
> > I will/shall sing   you will/shall go   they will/shall play
>
> Often this is *contracted* (shortened), to **I'll**, **you'll**, **he'll**, **we'll** or **they'll** – e.g. *I'll speak. They'll be late. You'll play.*
>
> **Shall** is often used for emphasis – e.g. *You **shall** go to the ball, Cinderella.*

Change the tense of the verbs in the sentences below to show that the events will happen in the future simple. Change other words, if necessary, to make sure your sentences make sense.

Example: The dog **is** at the vets today. The dog **will be** at the vets tomorrow.

1.   We go to Greece on holiday.

_____

2.   The school closes today.

_____

3.   We received our exam results last week.

_____

4.   The car goes in for a service today.

_____

> We also use the **present simple** in certain circumstances – e.g. **We fly** *tomorrow*. This suggests a future action, although the verb is expressed in the present tense.
> We can also say **We are going to** *do something*, again suggesting future action.

Future continuous tense

> The **future continuous** tense is formed by using the **future simple** of the verb **to be** (*will/shall be*) with the **present participle** (ending in '**-ing**') of the main verb.
>
> > **I shall/will be** coming   **we shall/will be** coming
> > **you shall/will be** coming   **you shall/will be** coming
> > **he/she/it shall/will be** coming   **they shall/will be** coming

Write a sentence of your own using the future continuous tense.
Example: I will be watching TV at six o'clock.

_____

DiaGram is published by Hodder & Stoughton Educational.
The publishers grant permission for photocopies of this sheet to be made for use solely in the purchasing institution.

30

DiaGram

Date _____

Name _____

Future perfect tense

The **future perfect** tense is formed by using the **future simple** of the verb **to have** and the **past participle** (ends in -**ed**, or irregular) of the main verb:

I shall/will have talked   You shall/will have passed   They shall/will have been

Write sentences using the verbs below in the future perfect tense, as shown in the example.

walk   finish   paint   clean   cry

Example: **I shall have played** guitar for an hour by the end of the gig.

_____

_____

_____

_____

Future perfect continuous tense

The **future perfect continuous** tense uses *two* auxiliary verbs: the **future simple** of **to have** (*shall/will*), the **past participle** of **to be** (*been*) and the **present participle** of the main verb:

I **shall/will have been** talking.   They **will have been** skating.

Underline the future perfect continuous of the verbs in these sentences.

1.   I will have been living here for two years in September.

2.   They will have been married for ten years on their anniversary.

3.   You will have been going to that school for as long as I did.

4.   They will have been walking for almost the whole day.

5.   They will have been on the court for a record length of time.

Complete these sentences by adding a suitable verb in the future perfect continuous tense.

1.   They_____ in the tree house by then.

2.   You _____ tea by the time they come.

3.   We _____ TV when you arrive.

4.   I _____ my homework by 8.00 p.m.

DiaGram is published by Hodder & Stoughton Educational.
The publishers grant permission for photocopies of this sheet to be made for use solely in the purchasing institution.

31

Verbs – tense

a) **Write the verb *to play* in the first person singular (I) and to be in the *third person singular* (he/she/it), in the present, past and future simple tenses.**

                           to play   *to be*

Present _____   *Present* _____

Past _____   *Past* _____

Future _____   *Future* _____

b) **Write the present continuous form of *to sing* in the *first person singular* (I).**

_____

c) **Write the past continuous form of *to dig* in the *first person plural* (we).**

_____

d) **Write the future continuous form of *to dive* in the *third person singular* (he/she/it).**

_____

e) **Write the present perfect form of *to build* in the *third person singular* (he/she/it).**

_____

f) **Write the present perfect continuous form of *to build* in the *second person plural* (you).**

_____

g) **Highlight or underline the *past perfect* and the *past perfect continuous* tenses in this passage.**

I had done too much homework. In fact, it seemed as if I had been doing too much homework for weeks. The exams had finished now, thank goodness. If I had revised properly all term, I wouldn't have been staying up to all hours trying to catch up. I had been a fool, but I have been trying hard to make up for my past laziness.

h) **Highlight or underline the *future perfect* and the *future perfect continuous* tenses in this passage.**

I shall have finished my tea by the time you are changed. You will have been getting ready to go out for two hours. I will have eaten, washed up and I shall still have taken less time than you've taken. It's a good job we're not in a hurry.

Verbs	Secure	Work Required
Tense	☐	☐

Adverbs

Adverbs (dictionary abbreviation *adv.*), as their name suggests, **add to the meaning** of verbs – e.g. *He ran* **quickly**, *She ate* **greedily**. They can tell us where *when*, *how* and *how often* the action of the verb occurs. Often, they end in **-ly**:

slowly   happily   madly   merrily   awfully   badly

Adverbs can be formed from nouns and adjectives:

abstract noun – beauty   **adjective** – beautiful   **adverb** – beautifully

Form adverbs from these nouns and adjectives.

quick _____   joy _____

shy _____   dainty _____

safe _____   careful _____

Adverbs are very useful for adding interest to speech and writing.

Look at the list of adverbs in the box and choose ones which fit into the spaces to complete the story. You will not need them all. You may use a word more than once.

slowly	carefully	lazily	merrily	carelessly	rapidly
meanly	crossly	daintily	safely	playfully	casually

Mavra got up _____ and looked at Scat who was lying in front of the fire which was blazing

_____. She moved towards him. Stepping _____ over the sleeping

cat, Mavra edged _____ towards the bowl of cat food tipped _____

onto the floor. Should she try to steal a mouthful? One look at the cat watching _____ from one

opened eye made the boxer dog think again. She moved _____ over to her toy left to one

side of the bowl. Picking it up in her strong teeth, she returned _____ to her own place by

the fire.

Underline the adverbs in this passage.

He moved slowly towards the strange object lying on the road. Was it alive? He touched it lightly with his foot. There

was no movement. Suddenly, a sound came from the parcel. Brr! Brr! Brr! What could it be? He looked thoughtfully

at it. Did he dare to open up the package carefully to see what was inside?

Adverbs – types of adverbs

The main classifications of **adverbs** are:

- adverbs of **time**: *when* something was done – e.g. yesterday, earlier, now.

- adverbs of **place**: *where* something was done – e.g. outside, nearby, up, far.

- adverbs of **manner**: *how* something was done – e.g. slowly, angrily, quickly.

- adverbs of **frequency**: *how often* something was done – e.g. sometimes, never.

- adverbs of **degree**: the *strength* of what was done – e.g. rather, very, slightly.

An adverb of degree can be used with another adverb:
    She **moved** *(verb)* **very** *(adverb)* **gracefully** *(adverb)*.
    He **did** *(verb)* **slightly** *(adverb)* **better** *(adverb)*.

Sometimes an adverb of degree is used to modify an adjective:
    The **rather** *(adverb)* **attractive** *(adjective)* girl was wearing a **very** *(adverb)* **pretty** *(adjective)* dress.

When a *phrase* does the job of an adverb, we call it an **adverbial phrase**:
    The idea came to him as **quick as a flash**.   *Quick as a flash* takes the place of *quickly*.

Make lists of adverbs under the headings below.

An adverb will have the letters *adv.* next to it in a dictionary, if you need to check you have the correct part of speech. Notice that some words act as *more than one* part of speech, depending on where they come in a sentence:

    This is the **very** *(adjective)* place. She sang **very** *(adverb)* happily.

time	*place*	*manner*	*frequency*
_____	_____	_____	_____
_____	_____	_____	_____
_____	_____	_____	_____
_____	_____	_____	_____

Complete these sentences with suitable adverbs.

1. The fox slunk_____ along the hedgerow.

2. The cold struck _____ as we stepped out into the night.

3. Parents often behave _____ towards their children.

4. Objects left _____ on stairs can cause accidents.

5. I laughed _____ as the clown stood in the bucket of paint.

DiaGram is published by Hodder & Stoughton Educational.
The publishers grant permission for photocopies of this sheet to be made for use solely in the purchasing institution.

Adverbs

Date _____

Name _____

a) Complete this sentence:

An adverb _____ a verb.

b) Write two examples of each type of adverb, using the headings as a guide.

time	place	manner	frequency	degree
_____	_____	_____	_____	_____
_____	_____	_____	_____	_____

c) Highlight the adverbs in the passage.

The bell clanged madly as I rushed breathlessly into the playground. Was I late? I really hated having to go and sign in the late book. The school secretary looked disapprovingly at you. It made me feel frighteningly small and useless. That look said it all. If I couldn't get to school on time, how would I ever get to work punctually?

What did she know about leaping out of bed, eating and drinking hastily then rushing off to do a paper round?

d) Choose a suitable adverb to fill the gaps in the passage.

I was _____ surprised when I saw you were still waiting _____ for me. I got up _____ when the alarm went off . I had _____ woken up before the alarm went off but I like to stay in bed _____ until the last minute. I ate my breakfast _____ and thought I had lots of time before setting off to school. Then I looked _____ at my watch. Where had the last half-hour gone? I was _____ sure that you would have given me up and stormed _____ away.

Adverbs	Secure	Work Required
Adverbs	☐	☐

DiaGram is published by Hodder & Stoughton Educational.
The publishers grant permission for photocopies of this sheet to be made for use solely in the purchasing institution.

T32/3

Adverbs – comparative & superlative

Adverbs have a **comparative** and a **superlative** form.

Comparative

When we compare *two* actions, we use the comparative form:
add the suffix -**er**, or put **more** in front of the adverb. It is always one or the other, *never both*.

> I got up **earlier** than you this morning.
> Sarah works **more neatly** than Ivan.

Superlative

When we compare *more than two* actions, we use the superlative form:
add the suffix -**est** or put **most** in front of the adverb.

> Shomir arrived the **latest** out of all the pupils in the school.
> The home team played **most enthusiastically** out of all the competitors.

Exceptions to these patterns of spelling are:

adverb	*comparative*	*superlative*
badly	worse	worst
well	better	best
little	less	least

Underline the comparative and superlative forms of the adverbs in the sentences below.

1. Jane is a good cook, but Gill cooks more creatively.

2. Susan did well in the exams, but her brother performed badly.

3. Many dogs wag their tails madly, but Mavra wags hers the most wildly of all.

4. The poetry competition had some excellent entrants, but one young competitor spoke the most movingly of all.

5. The young child built his sand castle more carefully than anyone else on the beach.

6. Who sings the most beautifully in this choir?

7. Who runs the fastest out of the team?

8. It was noticeable that Mary spoke more politely than the other pupils in the class.

9. 'This is the best written book I have ever read,' exclaimed Sam.

10. She always ate very little, but now she eats less than ever.

Write some sentences of your own to show that you understand the use of comparative and superlative adverbs.

_____

_____

DiaGram is published by Hodder & Stoughton Educational.
The publishers grant permission for photocopies of this sheet to be made for use solely in the purchasing institution.

34

Adverbs – comparative & superlative

Date _____

Name _____

a) Write the comparative and superlative forms of these adverbs

	Comparative	*Superlative*
fast	_____	_____
hard	_____	_____
slowly	_____	_____
loudly	_____	_____

b) Complete these sentences with the most appropriate form of the word in brackets.

1. I get up early but my brother gets up even _____. *(early)*

2. The boy worked _____ than his older brother. *(neatly)*

3. Peter finishes his work the _____ of everyone in the group. *(quickly)*

4. The clock struck the hour the _____ of any I have ever heard. *(loudly)*

5. Alisha jumped the _____ of all the competitors. *(high)*

6. I can run _____ than you. *(fast)*

7. He tied the rope the _____ of all the pirates. *(tightly)*

8. This medicine is _____ than the one I tried before. *(well)*

c) Correct these sentences.

1. I did worser in my exams than my cousin.

    _____

2. He sang louder of anyone in the choir.

    _____

3. You are the bestest teacher I know.

    _____

4. They say I'm the goodest footballer they've ever seen.

    _____

Adverbs	Secure	Work Required
Comparative/superlative	☐	☐

DiaGram is published by Hodder & Stoughton Educational.
The publishers grant permission for photocopies of this sheet to be made for use solely in the purchasing institution.

T34

Adverbs – spelling rules

An **adverb** tells you more about a **verb**. It *adds to* the meaning of the verb.
We can form adverbs from adjectives, but need to follow spelling rules to make the new word:

> **1.** If the *adjective* ends in '**-l**', you add '**-ly**' – e.g. usual (*adjective*), usually (*adverb*).

Form the adverb from these adjectives

1. casual _____
2. awful _____
3. beautiful _____
4. boastful _____
5. annual _____
6. cheerful _____

> **2.** If the *adjective* ends in '**-ll**', just add a '**-y**' – e.g. *full, fully*; *dull, dully*.

Fill in the missing word.

1. The metal shone _____.
2. Do you understand this _____?

> **3.** If the adjective ends in '**-y**', change '**y**' to '**i**' and add '**-ly**' – e.g. *cheeky, cheekily*; *happy, happily*; *merry, merrily*; *noisy, noisily*.

Fill in the missing words using the words in the list above.

1. The boy answered the teacher back _____.
2. The birds sang _____.
3. The party carried on _____.
4. The baby played _____ in the pram.

> **4.** If the adjective ends in '**-ic**', add '**-ally**'.

Look, say, cover, write and check the adverbs in the spaces below.

sarcastic _____   fantastic _____

One word which does not follow this rule is *public*. Write it out in the spaces.

public / publicly _____ / _____   _____ / _____

> **5.** If the *adverb* ends in '**-e**', the spelling may include the '**e**' or drop it.

Look, say, cover, write and check in the spaces.

true / truly _____   sure / surely _____   pure / purely _____

DiaGram is published by Hodder & Stoughton Educational.
The publishers grant permission for photocopies of this sheet to be made for use solely in the purchasing institution.

Relative pronouns

Date _____

Name _____

A **relative pronoun** is a pronoun which helps to connect or *relate* one part of a sentence to another. These words are all **relative pronouns:**

who   whom   whose   which   that   what

Underline the relative pronouns in the sentences below.

1. The door which leads into the garden is blue.

2. The boy whose bicycle was stolen is upset.

3. The teacher wanted to see the girl who had spoken.

4. I need to know to whom I should pay the money.

5. The girl who my brother is marrying comes from London.

6. He hated the boy who came top of the class.

7. The toy which is broken cannot be repaired.

8. The old woman who I met in the wood is strange.

9. He was sorry he bought the record which had an attractive cover because he didn't like the music.

10. The girl wanted to know what she was having for her birthday present.

Remember these rules!

Which is *never* used of people.
    Example: I like **toys** which make a noise. *(things = which)*

Who is *never* used of things.
    Example: I like **people** who are noisy. *(people = who)*
Who is used when the relative pronoun is the *subject* of a verb.

What must not be used in place of *which* or *that.*
    Example: Those are the cakes **that** I prefer. *(Never … the cakes what I prefer!)*

We can also use **whom** after a preposition or when it is the *object* of a verb.
Whom is not used very often in informal language, however.

Choose the correct relative pronoun to complete these sentences.

1. We searched for the boy _____ was missing.

2. They are the invitations _____ I bought today.

3. Those are the girls _____ threw the stone.

4. These are the team members _____ will play on Saturday.

5. This is the dog _____ bit the postman.

6. The man _____ house was burgled is very ill.

DiaGram is published by Hodder & Stoughton Educational.
The publishers grant permission for photocopies of this sheet to be made for use solely in the purchasing institution.

36

Pronouns – *I* and *me*

Date _____

Name _____

Many people have difficulty in using **I** and **me** correctly in some sentences.

Which of these two sentences is correct? Tick the correct answer.

1. Mum and *me* are going on holiday. _____   *2.* Mum and *I* are going on holiday. _____

The answer is *2*.

> To check your own sentences, ask yourself this question:
> *Can I form a new sentence for each person and pronoun, and it still makes sense?*
>
> > *Mum* is going on holiday. *I* am going on holiday. *Me* am going on holiday.
>
> You can soon tell which is the incorrect one!
>
> There *is* an occasion when you do need to use the *object* form of the pronoun (see sheet 12 if you have forgotten the object form). When the pronoun follows a **preposition**, you always use the object form.

Complete these sentences by using the appropriate pronoun.

1. Janet and _____ are going to the cinema.

2. Both Clive and _____ were eating ice-cream.

3. My friend and _____ go horse riding every week.

4. My father bought presents for my sister and _____.

5. It is too late for my brother and _____ to reach the theatre on time.

6. Between you and _____ , this film is boring.

> **Points to remember about pronouns:**
> - The verb must be in agreement with the subject. If the **subject** is singular, the **verb** will be singular – e.g. *Kalim* **is** *going to the cinema.*
> - If you use a **singular** indefinite pronoun (e.g. *someone, anything, each*), you must use a **singular** verb – e.g. *Someone* **is** *coming. Each apple* **has** *a worm in it.*
> - If you use a **plural** indefinite pronoun (e.g. *both, several, some*), you must use the **plural** form of the verb – e.g. **Both** *of them* **have** *long hair.* **Several** *boys* **were** *running.*
> - Don't confuse **whose** (interrogative pronoun) and **who's** (contraction of *who is*).
> - Don't confuse **its** (possessive pronoun) with **it's** (contraction of *it is*).

DiaGram is published by Hodder & Stoughton Educational.
The publishers grant permission for photocopies of this sheet to be made for use solely in the purchasing institution.

37

Pronouns

Date _____

Name _____

a) Highlight the relative pronouns in these sentences.

1. The boy, with whom I had the argument, has apologised.

2. The boy, who was always top of the class, received a certificate.

3. The dress, which was always too tight, has now split.

4. My parents, to whom I owe everything, are lovely people.

5. This is the house that we built.

- -

b) What job does a relative pronoun do in a sentence?

_____

- -

c) Use *I* or *me* to complete these sentences correctly.

1. Jean and _____ are going out on Saturday.

2. The decision to leave was between Isaac and _____.

3. Put the bag between Salim and _____.

4. Mum took Joe and _____ swimming.

5. Julie and _____ will make the dinner.

- -

d) Add a pronoun or a verb to complete these sentences correctly.

1. _____ was watching a film.

2. When _____ were small we were always playing with a train set.

3. Everyone_____ to be in the team.

4. They _____ making it in technology.

5. _____ were walking together in the park.

Pronouns	Secure	Work Required
Relative	☐	☐
I/me	☐	☐
Agreement of pronoun and verb	☐	☐

DiaGram is published by Hodder & Stoughton Educational.
The publishers grant permission for photocopies of this sheet to be made for use solely in the purchasing institution.

A **preposition** (dictionary abbreviation *prep.*) is usually placed before a noun or pronoun in a sentence. It shows the **position** of one thing in relation to another in **space** (e.g. *under, up, below*) or **time** (e.g. *before, after, since*).

Examples of prepositions

in	into	with	before	after	to
on	until	over	under	beside	at
of	behind	down	around	against	since
for	beneath	above	along	across	underneath
from	beyond	below	among	between	towards
through	near	up	amongst	off	upwards

Some prepositions can act as other parts of speech:

He looked **up** (*preposition*) at me. The word *up* relates to the **pronoun** *me*.
He got **up** (*adverb*) and went to school. The word *up* relates to the **verb** *got*.

Put a suitable preposition in the spaces in the sentences below.

1. The fairground was _____ the main road.

2. The crane lifted the girder _____ high into the air.

3. The bulldozer pushed the rubble _____ the wall.

4. The ship sailed _____ the harbour.

5. The computer information showed up _____ the screen.

6. Put the ingredients _____ the bowl.

7. The circus horses galloped _____ the ring.

8. They ran _____ the street.

9. The brave man lay _____ the elephant's foot.

10. The high wire was _____ the crowd.

Some prepositions are *phrases* or groups of words. They are called **prepositional phrases**. They come before a noun or pronoun:

Put it **on top of** the table.   Walk **as far as** the park.   I'll finish **in spite of** you.

Of and **off** are both prepositions. Some people use them together. This is wrong:

The boy took the money **off** (*of*) the table – the word **of** is not needed.

Complete these sentences with either *off* or *from*.

1. The teacher took the mobile phone _____ the pupil.

2. Mum took the pan _____ the stove.

DiaGram is published by Hodder & Stoughton Educational.
The publishers grant permission for photocopies of this sheet to be made for use solely in the purchasing institution.

38

Prepositions

DiaGram Date _____

Name _____

a) Describe the job a preposition does in a sentence.

_____

_____

- -

b) Highlight or underline the prepositions in these sentences.

1.   The dog ran around the field.

2.   Put the dishes under the shelf.

3.   Hang your hat on the hook in the hall.

4.   Do your piano practice after tea.

5.   Look through the window at the sunset.

6.   Will you sit beside me, please?

7.   Shall I sit under the tree?

8.   Before tea I watched television.

9.   My dog sleeps behind the chair.

10. I leaned against the fence.

- -

c) Use these prepositions and prepositional phrases correctly in your own sentences.

        beyond   against   in spite of   except for   as far as

_____

_____

_____

_____

_____

_____

Prepositions	Secure	Work Required
Prepositions	☐	☐

DiaGram is published by Hodder & Stoughton Educational.
The publishers grant permission for photocopies of this sheet to be made for use solely in the purchasing institution.

T38

Capital letters

Date _____

Name _____

What do capitals look like compared to lower case letters?

Write the capital and the lower case letters on the line underneath each group of letters. The *a* and *g* you see printed in books are sometimes a different shape to the letters you write by hand. Write them as you usually do in your work.

A a   B b   C c   D d   E e   F f   G g

_____

H h   I i   J j   K k   L l   M m

_____

N n   O o   P p   Q q

_____

R r   S s   T t   U u

_____

V v   W w   X x   Y y   Z z

_____

We use **capital letters** for:

- names of people, places and things: **J**ane, **P**eter, **L**eeds, **N**ew **Y**ork.
- the first letter of a sentence: **I**t is a lovely day today.
- the titles of books, plays and music: **T**he **R**ed **P**ony, **J**ack and the **B**eanstalk.
- the names of rivers, seas and oceans: the **R**iver **T**hames, the **N**orth **S**ea, the **A**tlantic.
- the letter *I* on its own: **I** am very busy working hard.

- -

Highlight the words which should have capital letters in these sentences.

i am going to have my music lesson today. i am supposed to be playing a piece from the musical cats. when i get

there i will be in trouble because i went to london on saturday and sunday and i haven't done enough practice.

DiaGram is published by Hodder & Stoughton Educational.
The publishers grant permission for photocopies of this sheet to be made for use solely in the purchasing institution.

39

The full stop .

A **full stop** is used to:

- **Mark the end of a sentence** – e.g. *The children played at being aliens.*

- **Show some abbreviations:**

> Not all abbreviations take full stops. We tend to use full stops when letters are missing from the *end* of words (e.g. Prof. = Professor), but not when the missing letters are taken from the *middle* (e.g. Doctor = Dr):
>
> My name is H. J. Smith. = My name is Henry James Smith.
> My birthday is on Jan. 2nd. = My birthday is on January 2nd.

You don't need a second full stop if you end a sentence with an abbreviation which has its own full stop – e.g. *I like citrus fruits: oranges, limes, etc.*

- **Show when a sentence is unfinished or tails off:**

> A row of three or four full stops, called an **elipsis**, is used to show when written speech tails off – as if the speaker is unable to finish what they are saying for some reason. The sentence is unfinished. Add a fourth full stop if the elipsis ends a sentence:
>
> 'I told Mrs Blossom what … . Oh! Hello Mrs Blossom.'

- **Remember** too that there is a full stop at the bottom of a **question mark** and an **exclamation mark**:

  Help**!** I'm falling.
  May I leave early today, please**?**

- Full stops may also be used in **figures**, as a decimal point (e.g. 5.5%, £1.50) and in times (e.g. 5.30 pm)

Place full stops correctly in this passage. You will need to alter some letters to make capital letters. Look at the example first:

> help can anyone help me I'm stuck in the lift hel
> Help! Can anyone help me? I'm stuck in the lift. Hel …

if you like animals, they usually like you it is important that you speak to them you must be confident and keep your voice soft but firm never make sudden movements near animals they don't like it

The Royal Society for the Prevention of Cruelty to Animals has to rescue animals because people buy without thinking of all the problems as well as the fun of owning a dog when a puppy chews a rug because he or she is bored, who is to blame get out you horrid little is the sort of abuse some puppies often hear make sure you think about all aspects of owning a pet before you are tempted to get one

DiaGram is published by Hodder & Stoughton Educational.
The publishers grant permission for photocopies of this sheet to be made for use solely in the purchasing institution.

40

Capital letters & full stops

a) Underline the words in the list you think should have capital letters.

island   james   happy   easter   rain   america   skate   winter   cinderella

iron   europe   eiffel tower   tennis   euston station   pencil   choir   corfu

- -

b) Underline the words in the sentences which should have capital letters.

we went to london to see a concert at wembley stadium for my birthday treat.

they had tickets for a play but i wanted to stay at home and read romeo and juliet.

- -

c) Write out this passage, putting capital letters and full stops where they are needed.

it was a beautiful day mum and dad decided to take the whole family, including dogs, to blackpool to spend the day on the beach as soon as we left, there was a loud bang

'oh' said dad 'we've had a puncture' dad called the garage because he couldn't undo the wheel nuts he was mad it took two hours for someone to arrive and change the wheel we set off again it started to rain, no – to pour the rain was so heavy dad had to stop the car what a day out

_____

_____

_____

_____

_____

_____

_____

_____

_____

_____

Capital letters & full stops	Secure	Work Required
Capital letters	☐	☐
Full stops	☐	☐

T39/40

Commas

Date

Name _____

Commas are used to:

- **Separate items in lists** – e.g. *When we go on holiday we always take sun screen, plasters, safety pins and a pack of cards.*

> In a list, it is not usual to put the comma before a conjunction.
> The word *and* is used instead of a comma.

- **Help us to make sense of sentences with more than one part in them, and to read them aloud more effectively:**

    With the police chasing the thief got away.
    With the police chasing, the thief got away.

    The dog who had been barking for hours fell silent.
    The dog, who had been barking for hours, fell silent.

- **Separate subordinate clauses from main clauses and other subordinate clauses** (see sheet 7). This helps to make the meaning clear and to make reading easier. You can take a breath when you see a comma. Don't use a comma to separate sentences which should be joined by a conjunction.

    The teacher who was always very kind gave Natasha a comforting pat when she explained that she was late because her mother was ill.

    The teacher, who was always very kind, gave Natasha a comforting pat when she explained that she was late because her mother was ill.

- **Separate more than one adjective coming before a noun:**

    He was a handsome, cheeky boy.

- **Separate numbers, in thousands:**

    1,000   10,000   100,000   1,000,000

Put commas in the correct places in the following sentences.

1. We went on holiday with my aunt uncle cousins and grandparents.

2. Dennis who is very shy hid when he was made to go to the party.

3. Flat to rent containing entrance hall one bedroom kitchen bathroom living room.

4. The husband in the opinion of Chief Inspector Plod was the murderer.

5. Although nobody else could see them Ethel knew the ghosts were there.

6. My neighbour won £6000000 on the lottery.

Write sentences of your own on the back of this sheet to show that you can use commas correctly.

DiaGram is published by Hodder & Stoughton Educational.
The publishers grant permission for photocopies of this sheet to be made for use solely in the purchasing institution.

41

The comma

a) Use commas to complete the punctuation of these sentences.

1. I would like to go out tonight if you come as well.

2. They are good friends even though they often argue.

3. The dog usually well behaved started barking madly.

4. You can go to the ball Cinderella providing you are home by midnight.

5. My favourite foods are chicken fish cherries peaches and good bread.

6. If we decided not to go running then we could swim.

7. Walking is good for you so we are told.

8. The surgery had appointments at five o'clock five fifteen five thirty or a quarter to six.

9. The cut was deep bleeding heavily covered in mud and I was sure in need of stitches.

10. The old man of whom many tales were told had an interesting face.

- -

b) Place commas correctly in these number sequences.

    3096   24300   103863   8974320   56743200109

- -

When do we use commas?

c) _____

Example: _____

d) _____

Example: _____

e) _____

Example: _____

f) _____

Example: _____

The Comma	Secure	Work Required
List	☐	☐
Phrase/clause	☐	☐
Meaning	☐	☐
Numbers	☐	☐

DiaGram is published by Hodder & Stoughton Educational.
The publishers grant permission for photocopies of this sheet to be made for use solely in the purchasing institution.

T41

The apostrophe of omission

When you miss out one or more letters in order to make it easier to say certain words, you use an **apostrophe of omission** to show that letters have been missed out. It happens when you miss letters off the end of a word. You omit the letter(s).

she has – she's	you are – you're
he had – he'd	we will – we'll
I am – I'm	we have – we've
did not – didn't	do not – don't
will not – won't	I had – I'd

Notice that the apostrophe is usually – but not always – put into the space left by the missing letter or letters. In some cases the **spelling** changes:

of the clock = **o'clock**   All Hallows Evening = **hallowe'en**   shall not = **shan't**

will not = **won't**   can not = **can't**   although = **tho'**   it was= **'twas**

Making use of the apostrophe, write these pairs of words in a shorter form.

1. I am _____
2. would not _____
3. she is _____
4. it is _____
5. I shall _____
6. he will _____
7. have not _____
8. could not _____
9. you will _____
10. has not _____

- -

is not   I have   they are   can not   should not   did not   will not   you are   we are   we have

Now write these contractions out in full. You will find clues in the box.

1. we've _____
2. I've _____
3. we're _____
4. they're _____
5. you're _____
6. can't _____
7. won't _____
8. shouldn't _____
9. didn't _____
10. isn't _____

DiaGram is published by Hodder & Stoughton Educational.
The publishers grant permission for photocopies of this sheet to be made for use solely in the purchasing institution.

42

The apostrophe of possession

> The **apostrophe of possession** is used to show that the item *belongs* to someone or something:
>
> Jane**'s** hat – The hat belongs to Jane.

Put the apostrophe in the correct place in the examples below.
Then write out what the phrase means, as shown in the example above.

1. Marks scarf _____

2. Jims jumper _____

Put apostrophes of possession in the correct places in the following sentences.

1. Jims sports bag was full of smelly socks.

2. We wanted to go for a walk but the dogs lead couldn't be found.

3. The gardens high wall stopped us from seeing in.

> Some names and singular words have the apostrophe *after* the 's'. This happens when the singular word ends in '-**s**'. A double '**s**' in this situation would be difficult to say:
>
> Mrs Stevens' car is blue.   Mr Jones' hat looks funny.   The apparatus' cost was too high.

Put the apostrophe of possession in the correct place in the phrases below.

1. Charles crown   2. James success   3. The shorts hem

> Most **plural** nouns end in '-**s**'. When you use the apostrophe of possession in a situation where **more than one** item or person is involved, you usually put the apostrophe **after** the plural '**s**':
>
> The boys' coats were filthy. The dogs' leads were all mixed up.
>
> Some plurals do not end in '-**s**' – e.g. *men, women, sheep, salmon.*
>
> When the plural does **not** end in '-**s**', use 's to show possession:
>
> The **men**'s dinner was ready. The **sheep**'s teeth were broken.

Put the apostrophe in the correct place in these sentences.

1. That schools hockey team nearly always wins the cup.

2. The singers songs were always a hit for them.

3. Les shirt was dirty and torn after the fight.

4. The dogs bones were left in the kitchen at the kennels.

5. The womens trip was spoilt when the bus broke down.

6. Julies favourite group is having a gig on Saturday.

DiaGram is published by Hodder & Stoughton Educational.
The publishers grant permission for photocopies of this sheet to be made for use solely in the purchasing institution.

43

Apostrophes of omission & possession

a) Write out these contractions in full.

1. I'm _____
2. you'll _____
3. he's _____
4. isn't _____
5. she's _____
6. we'd _____
7. o'clock _____
8. I've _____

b) Write the shortened form of the following.

1. would not _____
2. do not _____
3. they would _____
4. who is _____
5. you have _____
6. we shall _____
7. should not _____
8. I will not _____

c) Put apostrophes in the correct places in each of these sentences.

1. Joannas hat is red.
2. I would like to drive Peters car.
3. James hopes are high that he will win the competition.
4. The mens cloakroom was locked.
5. Rosas children all enjoy sporting activities.
6. The childrens favourite game was hide and seek.

d) Place apostrophes where they are needed in this passage.

Its a special day today. Im going out tonight because its James birthday. Were going to a restaurant for a meal. Well probably have a pizza or hamburger but it will be James choice.

I couldnt care less where we go. I enjoy celebrating anyones birthday. Mary will be coming and so will Darren. Theyd better not be late or well miss the film were going to see after the meal. Marys often late but it is usually her familys fault. Shes always in a hurry because she has to do lots of jobs before shes allowed out.

Apostrophes	Secure	Work Required
of omission	☐	☐
of possession	☐	☐

DiaGram is published by Hodder & Stoughton Educational.
The publishers grant permission for photocopies of this sheet to be made for use solely in the purchasing institution.

T42/3

Exclamation & question marks

Exclamation mark !

> We use the **exclamation mark** when we exclaim and show humour, surprise, pain or draw attention to something:
>
>   Help!   Woof!   Oh dear!

Question mark ?

> The **question mark** comes at the end of a sentence in which we have asked a question:
>
>   Have you put the kettle on?   Does your head ache?

Notice that there is a **full stop** at the bottom of each of these punctuation marks.
You don't need another one to mark the end of a sentence.

- -

Use a question mark *or* an exclamation mark *or* a full stop to complete these sentences correctly. (Some of the sentences are statements and do not require either an exclamation or a question mark.)

1. Help I'm going under

2. I don't like custard, do you

3. Attention Will the owner of car number XYZ 234 please move it

4. I asked Carl if he would put the heating on

5. Stop Dangerous road ahead

6. Are you ready to go out yet

7. Shall we go to the party or not

8. Ros was asked if she liked both the yolk and the white of an egg

9. 'Ugh Do we have to wade through all this mud '

10. Whizz The rocket streamed into the air

Write sentences of your own using exclamation marks and question marks.

_____

_____

_____

_____

Now read the sentences aloud. Use your tone of voice to show the effect of an exclamation or question mark in reading.

DiaGram is published by Hodder & Stoughton Educational.
The publishers grant permission for photocopies of this sheet to be made for use solely in the purchasing institution.

44

Exclamation & question marks

a) The punctuation has been missed out of these sentences. Put the correct punctuation mark at the end of each sentence. Then write a letter in the box at the end of each sentence to say whether it is a question (Q), an exclamation (X) or a statement (S).

1. What did you do at school today ☐
2. I asked her if she was feeling better ☐
3. The boy, unexpectedly, yelled 'ouch' ☐
4. Is lunch ready yet ☐
5. I was told that I would be in the First Team ☐
6. Sam! Sam! Save me ☐
7. It is late-night shopping on Friday ☐
8. Shall we go to the fair ☐

- -

b) Put an exclamation or a question mark in the appropriate places in these passages.

'Help ' The girl cried as loudly as she could. Would someone arrive in time to save her

'Help me ' She screamed in fear. The water was rising fast. Where was her brother

◆◆◆◆◆◆◆◆◆◆◆◆◆◆◆◆◆◆◆◆◆◆◆◆◆◆◆◆◆◆

'Ouch ' Dad exclaimed as the hammer hit his thumb for the second time. 'Why does it always happen to me I

must be the most unlucky do-it-yourself person in the world,' he muttered.

'Oh no ' The shelf he was fixing started to tilt. 'Will somebody please come and hold this up ' he yelled crossly.

'Why do you always make such a fuss when you do any little job ' cried Mum.

'Fuss Fuss What do you mean, fuss ' Dad replied.

'It's more a question of do-it-ourselves than do-it-yourself, isn't it ' said Mum.

Exclamation & question marks	Secure	Work Required
Exclamation mark	☐	☐
Question mark	☐	☐

DiaGram is published by Hodder & Stoughton Educational.
The publishers grant permission for photocopies of this sheet to be made for use solely in the purchasing institution.

Brackets

Brackets can be used to separate out **extra information** from the rest of the sentence. They always come in pairs, with the information we need to bracket *between* them. They are 'stronger' than dashes or commas, but are used in similar situations. We could take out the information in the brackets and the sentence which is left would still make sense:

> The boys (*or should I say men*) crowded into the small boat.
> Add a clove of garlic (optional).

The extra information may be a **reference**, such as a page number or dates:

> See information on dashes (sheet 46).
> You will find the answers at the back of the book (pages 59–62).
> Roman Britain (43–410AD).

If the words in the brackets are a **list, phrase or clause**, put the punctuation *outside* the second bracket:

> Into the pan went all the vegetables (carrots, leeks and parsnips).

If the words in the brackets are a **full sentence**, you put the punctuation *inside*:

> I don't like you going out without a hat. (I am quite bald, you know!)

Put brackets into these sentences where you think they are needed.

1. This was being naughty as Harry knew but he couldn't stop now.

2. Choose anything you like from the shop providing it costs less than ten pounds.

3. Delicate plants may need protection in the winter especially in the north of England.

4. I want you to go to the theatre at six o'clock make sure you are on time.

5. Check the meaning of the word in the dictionary if you have one, of course.

6. Hercules, a famous Greek hero as I'm sure you know had to do some terrible jobs.

7. We rushed to our seats we had season tickets as soon as the gates were open.

8. Perth Western Australia is a fantastic place to visit.

9. Some fruits we can see in some shops now pawpaw, rambutan, persimmon, etc seem strange.

10. Add 200g 8oz of plain flour.

Write a sentence of your own, using brackets correctly.

_____

_____

_____

DiaGram is published by Hodder & Stoughton Educational.
The publishers grant permission for photocopies of this sheet to be made for use solely in the purchasing institution.

45

The hyphen

Hyphens look like dashes but have different jobs to do. There is no space between the words and the hyphen. Hyphens are used in several ways – especially with prefixes, and to show that words are linked in some way:

- **in compound words, where two words are joined together** – e.g. *ten-pound note, second-hand clothes.*

- **in some expressions** – e.g. *do-it-yourself.*

- **when a prefix is used** – e.g. *multi-media, ex-navy.*

- **when two words are joined together to form a double letter which would look odd together** – e.g. *reelect / re-elect.*

- **between written numbers with more than one word** – e.g. *one-half, sixty-one*

- **to make meaning clear** – e.g. *recover / re-cover.*

- **when a word is split at the end of a line, a hyphen shows the rest of the word is carried on to the next line** – e.g. *I didn't want to go out, but Mum told me that exer-cise was good for me.*

The dash

A **dash** is usually slightly longer than a hyphen, usually has spaces before and after it, and looks like this – . It can be used instead of *brackets* or a pair of *commas*.

It has three main uses:

- **in pairs, to keep an idea separate from the rest of the sentence.**

  Charlie – a very pleasant person – is going to the match as well.

- **to separate a list of words, phrases or examples from a short introduction or a conclusion at the end of a sentence.**

  If you like flowers – roses, carnations and similar plants – come to see my garden.

- **to show a change of direction of thought in a sentence.**

  Thomas ate all the chocolates – but I don't care because he'll get fat, not me.

If the information comes at the end of a sentence, only one dash is required to separate it from the rest of the sentence.

Write out these sentences on the back of this sheet, putting dashes where you think they should go.

1. There is magic about magic which we shouldn't talk about.

2. Cabbages, spinach and sprouts all these can be grown in an English garden.

3. Time to read and revise this is what I need to be successful in exams.

4. The whole school including the staff came out to cheer on the team.

5. We'd had a great day out and the best the midnight feast was still to come.

Hyphens & dashes

DiaGram

Date _____

Name _____

a) **Rewrite the following sentences, putting in *hyphens* where you think they should go.**

1. My Mum said that we must be half baked to go out in this awful weather.

_____

2. The comedian told a joke about his father in law, not his mother in law.

_____

3. The half hour was up before we learnt how to hold the oars of the rented rowing boat.

_____

4. Do you prefer to live in a semi detached house or a terraced one?

_____

5. I would like to reform the scout troop; it was disbanded two years ago.

_____

6. The man made a half hearted attempt to get a second hand car.

_____

7. Pre school children can learn many useful things.

_____

8. It was only a short term solution.

_____

9. I use a non stick pan when I cook.

_____

10. I must recover that chair; it is very worn.

_____

b) **Show the correct places for *dashes* in these sentences.**

1. There was no need for proof he was a thief in the minds of the crowd.

2. All of them along with their belongings were herded into a room.

3. The weather was bad not unusual in this part of the world and the ferry was cancelled.

4. Johnson a harsh but fair judge was in court that day.

5. The furniture covered in dust sheets showed that the house was not occupied.

6. Enough of all this talk come in and have something to eat.

7. Tom made the excuse as if he needed one that he was growing and needed lots to eat.

8. The material a beautiful heavy silk fell to the ground in graceful folds.

9. The whole team large, small, old, young, fat, thin jumped with joy when they won.

10. Information secret information has been stolen.

Hyphens & dashes	Secure	Work Required
Dashes	☐	☐
Hyphens	☐	☐

T46

Speech marks – "..." or '...'

Speech marks are often called **inverted commas** or **quotation marks**. They are used to show when words are *spoken* and you are writing the speaker's exact words.

This is called **direct speech** (see sheet 48 for *indirect* or *reported speech*).

Speech marks are placed at the beginning and at the end of the spoken words, and can come almost anywhere in the sentence. They are always used in pairs: if you open speech marks, always remember to close them. They can be single or double (but don't change from one to the other in the same piece of writing). Notice that the opening and closing marks curve inwards towards the speech.

Speech marks are always used with other punctuation:

Capital letters are always used whenever somebody new starts to speak, or when you start a new sentence within the speech:

> Leo said, '**H**e is very happy today.'

Don't use a capital letter if you are continuing the *same* sentence following on from the 'saying' verb (unless it is *I* on its own or a proper noun):

> 'When,' asked Peter, '**d**id you start to prepare dinner?'

Commas are used between the words spoken and the 'saying' verb:

> 'I love watching football**,**' declared Cath.
> Janice screamed**,** 'Get away from me!'

Notice that other punctuation marks come **inside** the speech marks. Question marks and exclamation marks act as full stops, and don't need a comma as well.
When the 'saying' verb follows on from the question, use a lower case letter:

> 'Are you ready to go now?' **a**sked Maria.

You can put commas before and after the name of the person being spoken *to*:

> 'You know I hate going out in the rain**,** Jack**,**' commented Lisa.

Punctuate these sentences.

1. Philip whispered Janet I think there is someone peeping in through the window.

   _____

2. Can you be ready at six o'clock asked Susan.

   _____

3. Raspberries strawberries peaches and nectarines are delicious said Paula.

   _____

4. Will declared I'm going to be the top of the class.

   _____

5. I have won said Dad a million pounds in the lottery.

   _____

6. How cried mother did you manage that you said it was a waste of money.

   _____

DiaGram is published by Hodder & Stoughton Educational.
The publishers grant permission for photocopies of this sheet to be made for use solely in the purchasing institution.

47

Direct & indirect speech

Direct speech is the words actually *spoken* by someone. They are enclosed by **speech marks** (see sheet 47). Each new speaker begins on a new line:

> 'Shall we go shopping this afternoon?' Sarah asked.

> 'Do we have to?' Joseph replied.

It is always more effective to vary the 'saying' verb when using direct speech in a story, to make your work more interesting. Don't just keep using *said*. Think of such variations as *asked, replied, shouted, whispered, murmured,* etc.

Indirect speech is what is *reported* to have been said.

It is sometimes called **reported speech**:

> Joseph, when asked by Sarah if he would like to go shopping that afternoon, asked if they really must.

Notice that changing from direct to indirect speech *doesn't* mean that you simply miss out the speech marks. You need to be very careful about the **tense** (see sheet 23). There may be changes to time and person indicated – e.g. *I did / he/she/it was doing.* (It is a good idea to say each sentence to yourself before writing anything down.)

Change these sentences from direct to indirect speech.

Example: 'Bruce, would you like a drink?' Peter asked.
Bruce was asked by Peter if he would like a drink.

1. 'Try to bring the car home in one piece,' said Dad.

    _____

2. 'No excuses, Julie. You must make time to do your homework,' said the teacher.

    _____

3. 'I hate you!' yelled Samantha.

    _____

Change this indirect speech into direct speech.

1. She said that she would deliver the new chairs next day.

    _____

2. She demanded that she see the manager at once.

    _____

3. Jack insisted that he drive Janet home because it was so late.

    _____

4. He offered to collect the paper from the newsagents.

    _____

Speech marks, direct & indirect speech

a) Put speech marks in the correct places in these passages.

Where are you, John? Mum called. It's your turn to wash up. You promised to share the jobs with Rosa if I bought you a computer.

Coming, Mum, John answered without enthusiasm. I'll just finish this game.

John, I called you half an hour ago, Mum shouted angrily. If you can't keep your side of the bargain, that computer is going.

I give in, John said and trailed into the kitchen. Mums always win in the end.

◆◆◆◆◆◆◆◆◆◆◆◆◆◆◆◆◆◆◆◆◆◆◆◆◆◆◆◆◆◆◆◆◆

Hello. How are you? asked my uncle.

Fed up and hard up, I replied.

The trouble with you young people … he continued, listing the weaknesses of modern youth.

I'm sure you always spent your money wisely, I said to him.

I bet you've never had the fun I've had spending mine unwisely, I said to myself.

b) Put D for direct, or I for indirect speech, in the brackets at the end of each sentence.

1. 'I cleaned the car,' said Francis. (   )

2. Joan was reminded that her behaviour had been awful that day. (   )

3. 'I never seem to have enough time to finish my homework,' complained a pupil. (   )

4. She was reminded that it is necessary to create time for essentials. (   )

5. Paul told his wife that he was going to take the dog for a walk. (   )

6. He was told by the policeman to calm down and stop shouting. (   )

7. 'What time is the next train to Liverpool?' asked the traveller. (   )

8. 'Shall we try the jet-ski?' asked the tourist. (   )

9. We were told to fasten our seat belts securely on the plane. (   )

10. 'The weather is too rough to take a boat out,' said the fisherman. (   )

Speech marks, direct & indirect speech	Secure	Work Required
Speech marks	☐	☐
Direct/indirect speech	☐	☐

DiaGram is published by Hodder & Stoughton Educational.
The publishers grant permission for photocopies of this sheet to be made for use solely in the purchasing institution.

T47/8

Semi-colon & colon

Date _____

Name _____

Semi-colon ;

> A **semi-colon** is used to *link* together two or more *connected ideas* in a sentence. It marks a *pause* in a sentence and is *stronger than a comma* – but not as strong as a full stop:
>
> > He was usually late; never early.   Try to be kind; never sarcastic and spiteful.
>
> It can be used **in place of a conjunction** such as *therefore*, *nevertheless*, *besides*, although not usually ordinary ones such as *and* or *but*.
>
> Use a **semi-colon** when both clauses (parts of the sentence) are equal in importance:
>
> > I went to the market today; my usual Tuesday practice.
> > The lights went out; there was an expectant hush.

Colon :

> A **colon** can be used **before the start of a list**:
>
> > The boys were asked to bring: *sandwiches, a drink and a raincoat.*
>
> It can also be used to **introduce a quotation**:
>
> > He quoted: *'To be or not to be? That is the question.'*
>
> It is sometimes placed before a clause which defines or **adds extra meaning** to the first part of a sentence:
>
> > At last the truth emerged: *the boy had lied to save his sister.*

We don't use a **capital letter** immediately after a semi-colon or a colon unless it is the first word of a quotation or a name.

- -

Use either a semi-colon or a colon to punctuate these sentences. You will also need to think about commas and speech marks.

1. The engine spluttered into life stopped started again then it gave up.

2. The dog jumped through the hoop barked loudly then disappeared into the crowd.

3. To make a cake you will need eggs flour butter sugar and a strong arm.

4. I have four favourite foods prawns prawns prawns and prawns.

Write sentences of your own to show that you can use these two punctuation marks correctly.

_____

_____

_____

DiaGram is published by Hodder & Stoughton Educational.
The publishers grant permission for photocopies of this sheet to be made for use solely in the purchasing institution.

Semi-colon & colon

Date _____

Name _____

a) Place semi-colons in these sentences where you think they should go.

1. Some pupils are keen to make progress others prefer to make chaos.

2. The match was important everyone knew that.

3. He would need shirt, shorts and boots food for the journey money for his ticket.

b) Place colons in this passage where you think they should go.

We decided to form a gang. We had several lots of enemies the Clongs, the Wets and the Misfits. We had to choose the members of our gang from the following list Mary, Jasmin, Clive, Ranjit and Rohima. Bonkers, our leader, quoted the saying 'You can't make a silk purse out of a sow's ear.' The others weren't impressed they didn't know what it meant.

c) Place semi-colons or colons in the correct places in the following sentences.

1. The dancer was known as Flight a name which suited her perfectly.

2. In many films, the hero disappears into the sunset the music fades away.

3. I love coffee my sister prefers water.

4. The recipe is very rich and requires these ingredients a dozen eggs, 500g of chocolate, 250g butter, 250g sugar and half a litre of cream.

5. Mum's favourite quotation 'Fortune aids the brave.'

6. As a teacher I had one main aim for my class to be the happiest in the school.

7. I was late so I called a taxi the taxi rank is just round the corner from my house.

8. I was an actor working so hard I had no time for fun how could I change things?

9. My mother said to herself I will change the furniture round and I don't care what the family says.

10. For next term we need to order the following ten packs of pens, six reams of paper and some text books.

Semi-colon & colon	Secure	Work Required
Semi-colon	☐	☐
Colon	☐	☐

DiaGram is published by Hodder & Stoughton Educational.
The publishers grant permission for photocopies of this sheet to be made for use solely in the purchasing institution.

Paragraphs

Date

Name _____

A **paragraph** breaks up a larger piece of writing: each paragraph usually consists of several sentences about one particular topic or idea.

In **stories**, you start a new paragraph for a change of:

- **person**
- **place**
- **time**
- **idea**
- **action.**

In a **report** or piece of **formal writing**, it is usual to start a new paragraph for each **new point** being made.

Paragraphs may be either **blocked** or **indented**.

Blocking is usually used on formal letters or reports, particularly when they are written on a computer. The 'block' is formed by pressing the return key twice in order to leave a one-line space between the 'blocks' of writing.

An **indented** paragraph starts at a short distance from the margin. You continue your writing from the margin on the next line. It is not usual to miss a line between indented paragraphs.

Each paragraph should *start* with a sentence which **introduces the main idea**.

One or more sentences will *continue* to tell you **more** about the main idea.

The closing sentence should **lead** you on to the *next paragraph* or, if it is the final paragraph of a piece of work, **close** the subject with a suitable conclusion.

Read the following paragraphs.

Use different coloured pens and highlight or underline the sentences showing the three parts of each paragraph as described above.

Keeping pets is never easy. They need your time, energy, patience and often, quite a lot of money. How much of each of these things is required depends on the type of pet you choose. Take for example a dog.

A dog may become badly behaved if it is bored and lonely. You need to give it plenty of exercise depending on the age and breed of dog. Training dogs to behave well requires a lot of patience. All dogs need to have injections to protect them from disease and visits to the vet can be expensive. If you are unlucky and your dog has a health problem, this can increase costs considerably.

Is the expense and trouble worth it? In my opinion it is. I wouldn't be without my energetic, mischievous, time consuming, but loveable dog for a million pounds. Would you like to own a pet?

Is the passage above blocked or indented?   Answer _____

DiaGram is published by Hodder & Stoughton Educational.
The publishers grant permission for photocopies of this sheet to be made for use solely in the purchasing institution.

50

Paragraph planning

Write a **paragraph plan** before starting any long piece of written work. Jot down your ideas on the topic, then organise them into a sensible order, grouping them so that ideas which go together are in the same paragraph.

Here is a paragraph plan for a short essay entitled *Keeping Pets is Never Easy.*

Notice that a reminder about using a sentence to **link** paragraphs – so that each one leads into the next – has been included in the notes.

Para.1. What is the piece about?. What's involved in keeping pets. Example of dog. Linking sentence.

Para 2. How the things in paragraph 1 are true for keeping a dog. Relate to title: never easy. Linking sentence.

Para 3. Conclusion. Description of my pet. My opinion.

Write a paragraph plan for one of these titles.

My best/worst birthday   Football   Food   My family

_____

_____

_____

_____

_____

- -

Write a paragraph plan for a formal letter to a pet food company asking them to send you information on their products for a project you are doing.

Write your 'brainstorm' ideas, of points to include, first.

Points to include: Name of school, my name, age _____

_____

_____

_____

Paragraph plan

Para. 1 <u>Facts: name, school, reason or contacting them.</u> _____

_____

Para. 2 _____

_____

Para. 3 _____

_____

DiaGram is published by Hodder & Stoughton Educational.
The publishers grant permission for photocopies of this sheet to be made for use solely in the purchasing institution.

51

Paragraphing

a) **When should you start a new paragraph?**

_____

_____

_____

b) **Use ‖ to show where new paragraphs should start in this passage.**

What do you get from a day at school? Most people would say you go to have lessons but school is much more than that. Have you thought about these examples of what happens during a school day? You meet other people of different ages. You have to learn to get on with other people. You make decisions. You play and take part in sport. You learn to take instructions. Sometimes you have to do things you don't want to do and do them without being moody. These are lessons of a different kind to History and Science, but they are just as important. Think about what you have learnt at school today in addition to the lessons on your timetable. Make a list of your findings. I expect you will be surprised at how much you have learned without noticing.

c) **Write a paragraph plan for a piece of writing with the title Loud Music. Use the title and 'brainstorming' ideas to help you. Add ideas of your own.**

fun	deafness	Dad cross	ear plugs	ghetto blaster	Mum
dancing	neighbours	dog	favourite music	Rave	friend
party	school	youth club	night	lights	police	laughter

Para. 1 _____

_____

Para. 2 _____

_____

Para. 3 _____

_____

Paragraphing	Secure	Work Required
Paragraphing	☐	☐

DiaGram is published by Hodder & Stoughton Educational.
The publishers grant permission for photocopies of this sheet to be made for use solely in the purchasing institution.

Similes

We use **similes** when we want to **compare** one thing with another, in order to give us a clear picture of it. We choose something we know well, then say this thing is *like* another.

Usually we use the words **as** or **like**. Other words used in similes are **as if** and **as though**.

'As **b**lind as a **b**at' tells us that the person being described has no more vision than a bat. Most people know that bats have very poor eyesight, so it is a very powerful way of saying just how blind the person is.

This is a very useful device when you are describing a person, place or object.

We *transfer* the qualities of one thing to the other in our imagination.

We often use the same initial letter for the key words – as in the example above.
This is called **alliteration** (see sheet 54), and is a useful special effect.

Choose a suitable word from the box to complete these similes.

bat	charity/ice	grass	doornail/dodo	life	snail	berry	toast	doorpost
partridge	thieves	button	cucumber	flounder	Punch	pikestaff	ditchwater
peacock	kitten/water	crystal	fiddle	brass	rain/ninepence	bee

1. as cool as a _____
2. as large as _____
3. as busy as a _____
4. as plump as a _____
5. as fit as a _____
6. as pleased as _____
7. as clear as _____
8. as flat as a _____
9. as blind as a _____
10. as deaf as a _____
11. as proud as a _____
12. as thick as _____
13. as dull as _____
14. as bold as _____
15. as cold as _____
16. as brown as a _____
17. as plain as a _____
18. as slow as a _____
19. as weak as (a) _____
20. as warm as _____
21. as right as _____
22. as dead as a _____
23. as green as _____
24. as bright as a _____

Complete the following sentences with your own similes.

1. The white clouds looked like _____

2. Albert was as _____

3. Jane won every race in the school sports. She ran as fast as_____

4. Jumbo's laugh was as _____

5. When Chris swallowed the worm, he turned as _____

DiaGram is published by Hodder & Stoughton Educational.
The publishers grant permission for photocopies of this sheet to be made for use solely in the purchasing institution.

52

Metaphor

When **metaphor** is used, we say that one thing **is** or **was** another (i.e. not just *like* it), to help us describe something or someone:

> The moon **was** a ghostly galleon tossed upon cloudy seas.
> That child **is** a little monkey.
> Her hair **was** a river of silk.

In the *first example*, the poet says the moon was a ghostly galleon and the clouds were the sea, but we know that this is impossible. It does give a strong picture, though, of how the moon moved across the sky, because we know what a ship looks like when it is tossed about in a storm at sea.

In the *second example*, the child's behaviour is compared to that of a mischievous monkey. Again, most people are aware of how monkeys perform, and so we have a picture in our minds with which to compare the child's behaviour.

Explain the metaphor used in the third example.

_____

_____

_____

Underline the things being compared in these sentences.

1. His fingers were sausages of thick, pink flesh.
2. That boy is a little monkey; he's always in trouble.
3. The sun is a yellow ball in the sky.
4. The earth is a toy globe viewed from the moon.
5. The stars are fairy lights clinging to the dark velvet of the night.
6. The ground beneath the trees was a carpet of leaves.
7. The saw was a row of sharp teeth biting into the log.

Complete these metaphors.

1. The _____ was a mule in his stubbornness.
2. The girl was _____ in the way she spread gossip.
3. He was a/an _____ of a man.
4. The girl was a/an _____ she was so tiny.

Now make up some metaphors of your own.
Try to describe a dog, a car, a storm, your home, or your own choice of subject.

For example: Your room is a tip!   My cat is a lion of an animal.   Mother is a saint.

_____

_____

_____

_____

DiaGram is published by Hodder & Stoughton Educational.
The publishers grant permission for photocopies of this sheet to be made for use solely in the purchasing institution.

53

Alliteration, consonance & assonance

Alliteration is the repetition of a consonant sound to produce a particular effect. It is used in:

- tongue-twisters – e.g. **s**he **s**ells **s**ea **s**hells on the **s**ea **s**hore.

- advertising – e.g. **p**icked at the moment when the **p**eas went **p**op.

- poetry and other writing to make special sound effects – e.g. *I hear **l**ake water **l**apping by the shore.*

Assonance is similar to alliteration, but is the *rhyming* or *repetition* of *vowel* sounds. The sounds may come in the middle of the words – e.g. sm**oo**th, b**eau**ty.

   The b**oa**t fl**oa**ted around the m**oa**t.

Consonance refers to the repetition of *consonants* at the *end* of syllables:

   Be**st** of all is a cru**st** of hot toa**st** thru**st** into your eager fi**st**.

---

a) Underline or highlight examples of *alliteration* in this verse.

Mavra is a boxer dog.

A creature brave and bold.

She is her owner's perfect pet

Good with children and the vet.

But when it comes to sit, or stay,

She never does it right away,

She'd rather stray than stay.

b) Underline the examples of *assonance* in these lines.

The surfers in their youth and pride, curl and swirl and ride the tide.

The music's beauty soothed the pupil's mind.

The wind and waves soared and roared.

c) Underline the examples of *consonance* in these lines.

He made a jest.

It was a test.

To see if wit and mirth and joy,

Would waken up the stricken boy

From his deep and endless rest.

d) Now write some lines of your own using any of these special effects.

_____

_____

_____

_____

DiaGram is published by Hodder & Stoughton Educational.
The publishers grant permission for photocopies of this sheet to be made for use solely in the purchasing institution.

54

Onomatopoeia

> **Onomatopoeia** is the use of words which imitate sounds. We use them to produce an image of the sound we hear. The words can be verbs or nouns.
>
> **A boom** is an *abstract noun*. It is something we know exists even though we can't touch it. When we hear the word, we can imagine the sound.
>
> **To boom** is a *verb*. If a person is described as booming at somebody, we can imagine how they are speaking.
>
> Another name for these words could be **sound-words**:
>
> crash   cuckoo   hiss   bang   twitter   purr   whizz

Ono / mat / op / oe / ia is a difficult word to spell. Break it up into **syllables** as shown.

Look, say, cover, write and check using the syllable breaks to help you.

_____   _____

Highlight the words in these sentences which imitate sounds.
(You may need to find out the meaning of *mistral*.)

1. The thunder crashed and the lightning flashed across the stormy sky.

2. The sea bashed and buffeted against the seashore.

3. The mistral shrieked around the deserted house.

4. A gigantic bang came from the direction of the science laboratory.

5. The rain hissed on the metal roof of the shack.

6. The lawnmower rumbled across the grass.

7. The chain saw buzzed its way through the tree trunk.

8. The lion growled a challenge.

Complete these pairs of words by adding a sound-word.

1. Don't _____ the celery.

2. Let's _____ the cymbals.

3. The _____ of the gong.

4. The _____ of my tummy.

5. The _____ of a tiger.

6. The _____ of a train.

7. The _____ of a helicopter.

8. The _____ of a bee.

Now use the back of this sheet to write some imaginative sentences of your own, using onomatopoeia to strengthen your descriptions.

DiaGram is published by Hodder & Stoughton Educational.
The publishers grant permission for photocopies of this sheet to be made for use solely in the purchasing institution.

Personification

Date _____

Name _____

> **Personification** is a special kind of **metaphor** (see sheet 53), in which we say that something *inanimate* (without life), or an *animal*, has some quality that is **human** – we make it seem like a **person**.
>
> > The **sun peeped** through the window.
> > My **dog talks** to me, you know.
>
> This is impossible – the sun hasn't got eyes, can't see and therefore can't 'peep' – but the picture helps us to 'see' what is being described. The writer is comparing the effect of the sun at that moment to a human action. Strictly, it doesn't make sense, but we know what the writer is describing. We also know that dogs can't speak!

Underline or highlight examples of personification in these sentences. Write underneath what human characteristic has been used.

The rug walked across the floor.
walking: The rug moves, as if it had legs to walk on.

1. The sun smiled at me.

   _____

2. The houses slept in the afternoon sunshine.

   _____

3. Fear was alive in the captured prisoner.

   _____

4. The stars danced in the midnight sky.

   _____

5. Happiness sang in my heart.

   _____

6. The trees whispered their secrets to me.

   _____

7. The birds gossiped as they sunbathed on the telephone wires.

   _____

8. The lights winked from across the bay.

   _____

9. Fear stalked the night.

   _____

10. The cricket bat spoke of loving care.

   _____

- -

Write examples of personification for: *a tree, a car, love.*

DiaGram is published by Hodder & Stoughton Educational.
The publishers grant permission for photocopies of this sheet to be made for use solely in the purchasing institution.

Synonyms & antonyms

> **Synonyms** are words which are **similar in meaning**. An example would be:
>
> **dirt** – *grime, muck, smut*, etc.
>
> Thinking of synonyms is a good way to expand your vocabulary. You can find lists of synonyms in a **Thesaurus**. This is a book which lists words with their synonyms.

Write three synonyms for each of the following words. The first is done for you.

group <u>company band crowd</u>

1. happy _____

2. inexpensive _____

3. hidden _____

4. enormous _____

5. instantly _____

6. comfortable _____

7. pretty _____

8. friend _____

> Remember, synonyms help you to make your writing and speech more interesting by providing **variety**. When you write **direct speech** (see sheet 48), it is a good idea to find synonyms for **'said'** – e.g. *replied, answered, muttered, responded, whispered.*

See how many you can think of and write them below.

_____

_____

- -

> **Antonyms** are words which are *opposite* in meaning:
>
> rich / poor   young / old   sweet / sour   happy / unhappy
>
> Sometimes there are several words which could apply – e.g. **rich**: *poor, impoverished, penniless.*
>
> Antonyms are often formed by using a **prefix** such as **ir-** or **un-**, or by changing a **suffix** from, say, -**ful** to -**less** – e.g. *responsible/**ir**responsible, conscious/**un**conscious, harmful/harmless.*

Write examples of antonyms of these words.

reversible_____ painful_____ certain_____

DiaGram is published by Hodder & Stoughton Educational.
The publishers grant permission for photocopies of this sheet to be made for use solely in the purchasing institution.

57

Homographs & homonyms

> **Homonyms** or **homographs** are words which are **spelt alike** but have **different meanings**.
> The *pronunciation* is also usually (but not always) different, with the *stress* on different syllables:
>
> > I **row** a boat, but have a **row** with someone.
> > The **wind** was howling. I **wind** up the window in the car.
> > It is important that the local people **produce** their own **produce.**
> > I'll **ring** the shop about collecting her wedding **ring**.
>
> These words are sometimes called **homographs** because they are **written** with the same spelling. The word **graph** comes from the Greek word **graphtos**, which means *written*. This makes sense, because you **write** the same letters, but *say* them differently, depending on the meaning you want.

Choose any five of the following homonyms and use them in your own sentences to demonstrate the different meanings.

row   sow   read   lead   refuse   groom   tear   bound

content   permit   conduct   second   minute   invalid

Example: I **refuse** to do the tidying up. Clear up any **refuse** and take it home with you.

1. _____

_____

2. _____

_____

3. _____

_____

4. _____

_____

5. _____

_____

- -

Write down any other homonyms you can think of, on the lines below.

_____   _____   _____

_____   _____   _____

_____   _____   _____

DiaGram is published by Hodder & Stoughton Educational.
The publishers grant permission for photocopies of this sheet to be made for use solely in the purchasing institution.

58

Homophones

> **Homophones** are words which **sound** the same but are **spelt** differently:
>
> I like **sauce** on my food.
> The **source** of the river is in the mountains.
>
> The word **phone** comes from the Greek word **phonee**, meaning *voice*. This makes sense because the words **sound** the same but are *written* differently, depending on the meaning of the sentence they are used in.

Use the correct form of these homophones to complete the sentences.

hall/haul   waist/waste   caught/court   raw/roar   idle/idol   veil/vale   passed/past   shore/sure
flour/flower   staid/stayed   seen/scene   stationery/stationary   weather/whether   bore/boar

1. The coats were piled up in the _____.

2. It is wrong to _____ food when people are starving.

3. The case was to be heard in the Magistrates _____ .

4. My hands were _____ from the intense cold.

5. The Devil finds work for _____ hands.

6. The bride wore a long white _____.

7. I _____ my driving test first time.

8. Are you _____ you want to go out?

9. Measure out the _____ , butter and sugar.

10. I _____ out late and couldn't get either a bus or a taxi home.

11. There is a wonderful _____ in the film when the hero saves the heroine.

12. The _____ car was causing an obstruction.

13. I don't care _____ you want to go or not.

14. That man is a terrible _____ , he repeats himself endlessly.

- -

Write the partner to these homophone words as shown in the example.

coarse / <u>course</u>   peel/ _____   mist/ _____   leek/ _____

passed/ _____   some/ _____   bare/ _____   weather/ _____

source/ _____   brooch/ _____   aisle/ _____   bier/ _____

bridle/ _____   bawl/ _____   assent/ _____   paws/ _____

slay/ _____   steak/ _____   earn/ _____   tern/ _____

Colloquial expressions

Name _____

Colloquial speech is **ordinary conversation**. It is **informal** but not slang. It includes phrases which, through frequent use, have taken on accepted meanings.

For example, you may say that you are '*over the moon*'. Nobody would think you meant that literally and had jumped over the moon. The accepted meaning is that you are very happy about something.

Some **similes** (see sheet 52) and **metaphors** (see sheet 53) are used so often, they have become colloquial expressions – e.g. *I'm as free as a bird. He's a little monkey.*

Explain, in the spaces provided, what you understand by these colloquial expressions. Discuss them with your teacher.

Example: She's no spring chicken.
If you referred to a lady in this way, you would be comparing her to a young hen in the early months of its life. The lady is past the 'spring' of her life and is no longer young.

1. 'My heart was in my mouth as the enemy approached.'

   _____

   _____

2. It was raining cats and dogs / It was coming down stair rods.

   _____

   _____

3. We had to face the music when we were late home.

   _____

   _____

4. The boys were given a rocket when they were cheeky.

   _____

   _____

5. 'I feel a bit under the weather today.'

   _____

   _____

6. 'I must say, you're really on the ball.'

   _____

   _____

7. Charles is happy at work. He's a big fish in a small pond.

   _____

   _____

DiaGram is published by Hodder & Stoughton Educational.
The publishers grant permission for photocopies of this sheet to be made for use solely in the purchasing institution.

60

Cliché & pun

Cliché

> **Cliché** refers to a hackneyed, or **over-used**, phrase or idea. Some people are said to *'talk in clichés'*. This suggests that they don't really *think* about what they are saying: they simply repeat well-known phrases and sayings.
>
> For example, when someone has several unpleasant things happen to them, a cliché might be *'it never rains but it pours'*. If a person always appears to be fortunate, another cliché is *'he has the luck of the devil'*. Many **colloquial expressions** and **figures of speech** have become clichés.

Underline the words which form clichés in these sentences.

1. Some people rely on brute strength and ignorance to win an argument.
2. My daughter thinks that money grows on trees.
3. He says he can't work because of his back, but he would say that, wouldn't he?
4. Don't worry, he'll be as right as rain in a minute.
5. It's all one to me. I don't care what happens.
6. My husband always says that nobody can cook like his mother.
7. 'Hello, hello, hello,' said the policeman. 'What have we here?'
8. 'Boys will be boys,' said Mrs Jones when her son broke my window.
9. 'There's no smoke without fire,' said the gossip.
10. 'It's six of one and half a dozen of the other,' said the teacher when he found two pupils fighting.

Pun

> A **pun** makes a humorous use of a word to suggest two meanings at the same time. Sometimes **homophones** play a part in making a pun. A person's name or job may be associated with a pun:
>
>> The couple, whose surname is **Harty,** are well known for being **hearty** eaters and enjoying a joke. They were **Harty** by name and **hearty** by nature.
>
> A shoemaker, say, might have puns made about soles, feet or leather.

Complete these puns using the words listed below.

> waist   Bean   soul   Ding Dong   fisherman   plumber

1. 'Where have you been?' said Mr _____.
2. 'I am the _____ of discretion,' said the fishmonger.
3. Miss Bell's nickname was _____ _____.
4. 'I'm having a whale of a time,' said the _____ to his friend.
5. 'I am wasting away,' said the girl when she measured her _____.
6. 'I'm putty in your hands,' said the _____ to his girlfriend.

DiaGram is published by Hodder & Stoughton Educational.
The publishers grant permission for photocopies of this sheet to be made for use solely in the purchasing institution.

61

Rhyme & rhythm

Rhyme

Rhyme is the repetition of **similar sounds** in words. The device is often, but not always, used in poetry – usually at the end of lines.

Sometimes the letter cluster making the similar sound is the same – e.g. pl**ane** / m**ane.** Sometimes it is quite different, although the sound is the same – e.g. w**eight** / l**ate.**

Rhyme makes lines easier to remember, because we can guess what word is likely to complete the rhyming pattern.

Read this verse aloud and listen to the sound of the words in bold. Notice that the rhyming words have the same letter clusters of a vowel and consonants. (We sometimes call word endings like these *rimes*.)

> Jo and Jack were down in the d**umps.**
> That was because they'd had the m**umps.**
> **Lumps** and **bumps,** their throats were th**ick,**
> and all the time, they felt quite s**ick.**

Now read these two lines aloud. Listen to the sounds made by the words in bold. Notice how these words are spelt. Here the *sound* is the same but the *spelling* differs.

> That's why we're **here**, to bring you some **cheer.**
> Now I've upset you. Oh **dear**! Oh **dear**!'

Listen to some rap music to hear some much more complex rhymes!

Write a list of words which rhyme with the word at the top of each column.

car	mouse	dangle	head	fear
_____	_____	_____	_____	_____
_____	_____	_____	_____	_____
_____	_____	_____	_____	_____

Rhythm

Rhythm is a pattern of *movement*. It is found in music and poetry. In poetry, the movement is obtained by the number of syllables in each line and the stress, or emphasis, placed on certain syllables and words. Read this verse aloud. Stress (say a little louder), the words in bold. Listen to the 'movement' suggested by the pattern of stresses. Fast rhythms suggest movement, slow rhythms suggest something more gentle:

> Scat **pulled,** the string **stretched.**
> He sprinted round the **tree.**
> He made the string **tight** with all his **might.**
> The thief would not get **free.**

DiaGram is published by Hodder & Stoughton Educational.
The publishers grant permission for photocopies of this sheet to be made for use solely in the purchasing institution.

62

Repetition & exaggeration

Repetition

> **Repetition** means to say or do something **more than once**.
>
> You have probably been told *not* to repeat yourself when you are writing about something. Usually, for example, you are told to use a **variety** of 'saying' words (*replied*, *answered*, etc) instead of just *said*, when writing direct speech; and **not** to keep writing *nice*, *so* or *well* in all your stories.
>
> There are occasions, however, when it **is** correct to repeat yourself, to create a 'special effect'. This can be done in both poetry and prose:
>
> > **'Get down! Get down!'** conveys a sense of urgency greater than saying it once.
> > **'I won't, I won't…'** is a very definite statement made stronger by repetition.
>
> You might use this form of speech when you are writing a story.

**Write two sentences using repetition to create an effect.
Pretend you are a soldier at war or a parent worried about a child.**

_____

_____

_____

_____

Read the poem the *The Highwayman*, by Alfred Noyes. Repetition is used in every verse. Think about why the poet did this. Do you think it works? Talk about it with a friend or your teacher.

Exaggeration

> **Exaggeration** means to make something **seem bigger** than it really is, and is another 'special effect' which can be used to make a point. A good example of exaggeration can be seen in the poem *The Lesson*, by Roger McGough. Here the behaviour of a teacher is so extreme that it is funny, but also makes a point about discipline in the classroom.
>
> We often exaggerate when we are telling a story to make what we say appear more interesting. The tale of *'the fish that got away'* is a popular story in which anglers tell of a huge fish they *almost* caught. They can't show it to you, because it got away.

**Make up a story of your own where somebody exaggerates the truth.
Write a paragraph plan of the plot.**

_____

_____

_____

_____

_____

DiaGram is published by Hodder & Stoughton Educational.
The publishers grant permission for photocopies of this sheet to be made for use solely in the purchasing institution.

63

Imported language

English is a language which contains words borrowed from many other languages – especially from Latin and French, but also from Celtic, Greek, Anglo-Saxon, Nordic, etc.

Words from many other countries have entered the English language – people who come from or have lived for a long time in another country bring back words which have gradually become part of English. We no longer think of words like *pyjama* or *spaghetti*, say, as foreign. Some imported words and phrases are used often, but not everyone knows what they mean, or where they come from.

Read the words and their meanings aloud. Discuss them with a teacher if you can. Now use them to complete the sentences below.

ad infinitum – forever – without limit. *(Latin)*
au revoir – goodbye / until we meet again. *(French)*
gourmet – someone who enjoys the best food and drink. *(French)*
post mortem – the examination of a body after death by doctors. *(Latin)*
status quo – something which keeps the same position. *(Latin)*
encore – when an audience asks a performer to repeat something. *(French)*
en masse – all together. *(French)*
vice versa – the other way round. *(Latin)*
en route – on the way somewhere. *(French)*
fait accompli – something which has been done and cannot be argued against. *(French)*
faux pas – an offence against usual social behaviour. *(French)*
hors d'oeuvres – items of food served as a first course. *(French)*
tête-à-tête – a private conversation between two people. *(French)*
curriculum vitae – brief account of one's career. *(Latin)*
ad lib – as one pleases. *(Latin)*

1. The audience shouted for an _____ after the concert.

2. We went out _____ _____ to see the film; ten of us in total.

3. The situation remained at a _____ _____ despite the riots.

4. I pass my friend's house _____ _____ to school.

5. The French assistant said, '_____ _____' when he left.

6. I think I made a _____ _____ when I asked Mary why she wasn't coming to the party.

7. The doctor carried out a _____ _____ on the victim.

8. Her voice goes on and on _____ _____.

9. Harry is quite a _____, he loves good food and wine.

10. I was asked to provide a _____ _____ when I applied for a job.

11. It is a _____ _____. I've left the firm.

12. The actor forgot his lines and had to _____ _____.

Standard & non-standard English

A news report…

'Two tourists were kidnapped from their holiday villa last night. It is believed that they are being held hostage by terrorists.'

Two people talking about the news report….

'Eh! Did you 'ear? A pair of geezers on holiday was grabbed by some thugs and are banged up somewhere wiv them as 'ostages.'

Standard English is the description given to the sort of English people use in **formal** writing and talking (even if it is spoken with an accent). Official letters from the council or school, newspapers, most radio and television announcements and similar forms of communication are given in Standard English.

Non-standard English is used by many people of all ages in everyday speech. It includes **slang**, a language people make up for themselves. Cockney rhyming slang is a good example of this: *'up the apple and pears'* means *'up the stairs'*. Some slang words – such as *quid* for £1 and *bloke* for a man – have become a part of everyday speech. Other words such as *blag* – meaning a robbery – may be less well known.

People in different parts of the country use different slang words for the same thing. Money may be called *dosh, dough, a wedge, the readies* – depending on where you are.

Non-standard English includes **lazy speech** where people don't finish words – e.g. *Where have you been?* **Where've ya bin?**   *Yes.* **Yeh**.   *You what?*   **Yer wha?**

Double negatives could also be included in the description, because it is a form of speech which doesn't make sense – e.g. *I* **don't** *want* **no** *tea*. This actually means that you *would* like some tea. Think about it!

Write a scripted conversation between two friends describing their weekend. Use non-standard English. Set it out as shown.

Speaker 1 Where ya bin Satday?

Speaker 2 _____

_____

_____

_____

_____

_____

_____

_____

DiaGram is published by Hodder & Stoughton Educational.
The publishers grant permission for photocopies of this sheet to be made for use solely in the purchasing institution.

65

Answers

Worksheets

1 Simple sentences
1. cut, *2.* play, *3.* watched, *4.* ran, *5.* sings, *6.* cooked.

2 Compound sentences
1. The boy… **as/while/when** … to school. *2.* The elephant…**because it**…was hungry. *3.* You can… **or**… tomorrow. *4.* He can juggle…**and**…tIme. *5.* I washed… **because**…treat. *6.* I clean… **after**…breakfast. *7.* You… **and/or**…later. *8.* I will…**if**… goal.

3 Complex sentences
1. A new girl, whose name is Maria, came to school today and is in my class. *2.* The bag, which contained the missing items, was recovered by the police today. *3.* The new shop, from which I bought my first computer, has now closed down.
4. I am writing to my aunt, who lives in France, to thank her for letting us stay with her on holiday.

4 Interrogative & imperative
Any sentences which ask a question. Any command or 'imperative'.

5 Conjunctions
and/because, because, while, after, until, but, and.

6 Connectives
1. I like … **but**…chips. *2.* The sky… **because**… raging. *3.* We will … **as soon as** …work. *4.* I am … **as long as** … best.
5. I will … **however** … week. *6.* They hurried … **so that** …rain.

7 Phrase & clause
1. C, *2.* P, *3.* C, *4.* C, *5.* C, *6.* P, *7.* P, *8.* P, *9.* C, *10.* P.

8 Common nouns & articles
wave, snake, bed, moon, church, bell, spade, seat, dog, egg.
Any common nouns which make sense in context.
1. an, *2.* a – an – a, *3.* an, *4.* an – the.

9 Proper nouns
Any proper noun which fits the category.

10 Abstract nouns
calmness, hope, life, anger, journey, joy, mildness, patience, holiday, heat, colour, hope, greed, hunger, happpiness, grief, calm.
1. beauty, *2.* patience, *3.* time, tide, *4.* work.

11 Collective nouns
1. herd, *2.* litter, *3.* fleet, *4.* pride, *5.* suite, *6.* gang, *7.* set, *8.* pack, *9.* gang/class, *10.* school.
1. anthology, *2.* convoy, *3.* shoal, *4.* congregation, *5.* volley, *6.* brood, *7.* company, *8.* queue, *9.* constellation, *10.* squadron,
11. choir, *12.* flight, *13.* swarm.

12 Pronouns: subject/object
1. I. *2.* you, I. *3.* I.
1. my, her, she, them. *2.* You, me. *3.* they, them, they.

13 Types of pronouns
Group 3: *yours, mine*. Group 4: *himself/Simon, herself/Jo*. Group 5: *What, whom*.

14 Singular & plural
1. The *dogs* wanted *their dinners*. *2.* The *children* had pet *mice*. *3.* *We* went to the *shops* to buy *loaves* of bread. *4.* The *babies were* crying for *their mothers*.

15 Adjectives – describing

horrible, Billowing, stinging, freezing, adventurous, long, weary, emergency, extra, warm, waterproof, bleak, Thorough, three, missing, frantic, bright, blue, frightening, blinding, short, steep, stone strewn, eight.

16 Adjectives – comparing

taller, tallest, higher, highest, smaller, smallest, worst, better, worse, better.

17 Adjectives – possessive

1. your, *2.* my, *3.* his/her, *4.* his/her, *5.* its, *6.* your, *7.* their, *8.* our, *9.* her, *10.* his.

18 Finite & non-finite

1. James, fell, *2.* aeroplane, flew, *3.* ship, sank, *4.* gardener, mowed.
1. To walk, *2.* Playing, *3.* Sleeping, *4.* To fight, *5.* to play, *6.* Playing, *7.* To swing, *8.* Eating.

19 Verbs – participles

running/ran, playing/played, jumping/jumped, fighting/fought, killing/killed, knitting/knitted, speaking/spoken, growing/grown, flying/flown.

20 Auxiliary verbs – to be & to have

1. I *will* be, *2. We ought* to do, *3. We shall* be, *4. We could* see, *5. I can* run, *6. I am* coming, *7. We have* been, *8. He may* be, *9. I am* going, *10. They couldn't* sing.

21 Auxiliary verbs – to do

1. does, *2.* does/doesn't, *3.* doesn't/does, *4.* do/does, *5.* Do, *6.* Don't, *7.* done, *8.* doesn't/do, *9.* done, *10.* did.

22 Verbs – active & passive voices

1. The huge black spider was eaten by the cat. *2.* The car is cleaned by Rosa every week. *3.* The money was hidden under the bed by the burglars. *4.* The rubbish was thrown into the bin by Julian. THE DOOR MUST BE CLOSED

23 Verbs – tenses

coming, know, get to sleep, had, sleep, said, be, talked, talked, keeping, promised, would be, to promise, to keep, sighed, works, is, doesn't, is giving, will be, make, behave, will go, are asked, put, put, have, are going, seems, asking.

24 Verbs – present tense

1. I am crying, he is crying, we are crying.
2. I am jumping, he is jumping, we are jumping.
3. I am singing, he is singing, we are singing.
4. I am dancing, he is dancing, we are dancing.

25 Verbs – present perfect & perfect continuous

Example: I have laughed, you have laughed, he/she has laughed, we have laughed, you have laughed, they have laughed.
You have been playing, I have been training, You have been getting, I have been running, You have been imagining.

26 Verbs – past tense

1. I laughed, *2.* We climbed, *3.* Kate jumped, *4.* Philip worked, *5.* I dropped, *6.* We cooked, *7.* We played.
1. I was going, *2.* was boiling, *3.* was flying, *4.* was walking, *5.* was digging.

27 Verbs – irregular past simple 1

Any sentences which show the correct irregular past version of the verbs indicated.

28 Verbs – irregular past simple 2

1. lit, *2.* flew, *3.* sold, *4.* read, *5.* paid, *6.* was, *7.* swam, *8.* spoke, *9.* had, *10.* gave, *11.* hung, *12.* sang.
1. taught, *2.* fell, *3.* began, *4.* hid, *5.* stood, *6.* did, *7.* froze, *8.* wore, *9.* did, *10.* sat, *11.* broke, *12.* grew, *13.* hung, *14.* sold, *15.* was.

29 Verbs – past perfect & past perfect continuous

1. had jumped, *2.* had played, *3.* had ridden, *4.* had skimmed, *5.* had floated.
1. had been going, *2.* had been boiling, *3.* had been flying, *4.* had been walking, *5.* had been going, *6.* had been running, *7.* had been promising.

30 Verbs – future: simple & continuous

1. We will go to… *2.* The school will close… *3.* We will receive… next… *4.* The car will go…

31 Verbs – future perfect & future perfect continuous

Sentences which demonstrate the use of 'shall have…'

1. I will have been living… *2.* You will have been married. *3.* You will have been going… *4.* They will have been walking…
5. They will have been…
1. …will have been playing… *2.* … will have been cooking… *3.* …will have been watching… *4.* will have been doing…

32 Adverbs

quickly, shyly, safely, joyfully, daintily, carefully.
lazily/slowly, merrily, carefully/rapidly/casually, carefully/daintily, carelessly, meanly/balefully/crossly, casually/playfully,
safely/crossly.
slowly, lightly, suddenly, thoughtfully, carefully.

33 Adverbs – types of adverbs

Time: now, tomorrow, soon, sometime, later, yesterday, before, etc.
Place: on, away, close, inside, outside, upwards, upside-down, behind, etc.
Manner: lightly, forcefully, prettily, huffily, charmingly, meanly, playfully, etc.
Frequency: always, often, rarely, frequently, annually, weekly, daily, hourly, etc.
1. guiltily/slyly/rapidly/silently, *2.* bitterly/sickeningly/sharply, *3.* lovingly/crossly/protectively, *4.* carelessly,
5. loudly/uproariously/unrestrainedly

34 Adverbs – comparative & superlative

1. more creatively, *2.* badly, *3.* most wildly, *4.* most movingly, *5.* more carefully, *6.* most beautifully, *7.* fastest, *8.* more politely,
9. best written, *10.* less.

35 Adverbs – spelling rules

1. casually, *2.* awfully, *3.* beautifully, *4.* boastfully, *5.* annually, *6.* cheerfully. *1.* dully, *2.* fully.
1. cheekily, *2.* merrily, *3.* noisily, *4.* happily.

36 Pronouns – relative

1. which, *2.* whose, *3.* who, *4. to* whom, *5.* who, *6.* who, *7.* which, *8.* who, *9.* which, *10.* what.
1. who, *2.* which, *3.* who, *4.* who, *5.* that, *6.* whose.

37 Pronouns – I & me

1. I, *2.* I, *3.* I, *4.* me, *5.* I, *6.* me.

38 Prepositions

1. near/across, *2.* up, *3.* over, *4.* into, *5.* on, *6.* into, *7.* around, *8.* across/along, *9.* under, *10.* above.
1. from, *2.* off.

39 Capital letters

I am going to have my music lesson today. **I** am supposed to be playing a piece from the musical **Cats**. **When I** get there **I** will be in trouble because **I** went to **London** on **Saturday** and **Sunday** and **I** haven't done enough practice.

40 The full stop

If you like animals, they usually like you. **It** is important that you speak to them. **Y**ou must be confident and keep your voice soft, but firm. **N**ever make sudden movements near animals. **T**hey don't like it.
The Royal Society for the Prevention of Cruelty to Animals has to rescue animals because people buy without thinking of all the problems, as well as the fun of owning a dog. **W**hen a puppy chews a rug because he or she is bored, who is to blame**?** **G**et out you horrid little **…** is the sort of language some puppies often hear. **M**ake sure you think about all aspects of owning a pet before you are tempted to get one**.**

41 Commas

1. We went on holiday with my aunt, uncle, cousins and grandparents.
2. Dennis, who is very shy, hid when he was made to go to the party.
3. Flat to rent containing: entrance hall, one bedroom, kitchen, bathroom, living room.
4. The husband, in the opinion of Chief Inspector Plod, was the murderer.
5. Although nobody else could see them, Ethel knew the ghosts were there.
6. My neighbour won £6,000,000 on the lottery.

42 The apostrophe of omission

1. I'm, *2.* wouldn't, *3.* she's, *4.* it's, *5.* I'll, *6.* he'll, *7.* haven't, *8.* couldn't, *9.* you'll, *10.* hasn't.
1. we have, *2.* I have, *3.* we are, *4.* they are, *5.* you are, *6.* can not, *7.* will not, *8.* should not, *9.* did not, *10.* is not.

43 The apostrophe of possession

1. Mark's scarf – The scarf belonging to Mark.
2. Jim's jumper – The jumper belonging to Jim.
1. Jim's sports bag was full of smelly socks.
2. We wanted to go for a walk but the dog's lead couldn't be found.
3. The garden's high wall stopped us from seeing in.
1. Charles' crown. *2.* James' success. *3.* The shorts' hem.
1. That school's hockey team nearly always wins the cup.
2. The singers' songs were always a hit for them.
3. Les' shirt was dirty and torn after the fight.
4. The dog's/dogs' bones were left in the kitchen at the kennels.
5. The women's trip was spoilt when the bus broke down.
6. Julie's favourite group is having a gig on Saturday.

44 Exclamation & question marks

1. Help!… *2.* … do you? *3.* Attention!…. *4.* full stop *5.* Stop!…. *6.* …yet? *7.* not? *8.* full stop. *9.* Ugh!…. mud? *10.* Whizz!.

45 Brackets

1. (as Harry knew), *2.* (providing…pounds), *3.* (especially…England), *4.* (make…time),
5. (if…course), *6.* (as I'm sure you know), *7.* (we had season tickets), *8.* (Western Australia),
9. (pawpaw …, etc.), *10.* (8oz),

46 Hyphen/dash

1. There is magic about – magic which …. *2.* Cabbages, spinach, and sprouts – all these…. *3.* Time to read and revise – this is…. *4.* The whole school – including the staff – came…. *5.* We'd had a great day and the best – the midnight feast – was still to come.

47 Speech marks

1. 'Philip,' whispered Janet, 'I think there is someone peeping in through the window.'
2. 'Can you be ready at six o'clock?' asked Susan.
3. 'Raspberries, strawberries, peaches and nectarines are delicious,' said Paula.
4. Will declared, 'I'm going to be the top of the class.'
5. 'I have won,' said Dad, 'a million pounds in the lottery.'
6. 'How,' cried mother, 'did you manage that? You said it was a waste of money.'

48 Speech marks & direct & indirect speech

1. Dad asked/requested that the car be brought home in one piece.
2. Julie was told by her teacher that she must make time to do her homework and not make excuses.
3. Samantha shouted that she hated me.
1. 'I will deliver the new chairs tomorrow,' she said.
2. 'I demand to see the manager at once,' she said.
3. 'Janet, it is late. I will drive you home,' Jack insisted.
4. 'I will collect the paper from the newsagents,' he offered.

49 Semi–colon & colon
   1. The engine spluttered into life; stopped, started again, then it gave up.
   2. The dog jumped through the hoop; barked loudly, then disappeared into the crowd.
   3. To make a cake you will need: eggs, flour, butter, sugar and a strong arm.
   4. I have four favourite foods: prawns, prawns, prawns and prawns.

50 & 51 Paragraphs/paragraph planning Teacher judgement required.

52 Similes
   1. cucumber, *2.* life, *3.* bee, *4.* partridge, *5.* fiddle, *6.* Punch, *7.* crystal, *8.* flounder, *9.* bat, *10.* doorpost, *11.* peacock, *12.* thieves, *13.* ditchwater, *14.* brass, *15.* charity/ice, *16.* berry, *17.* pikestaff, *18.* snail, *19.* kitten/water, *20.* toast, *21.* rain/ninepence, *22.* doornail/dodo, *23.* grass, *24.* button.

53 Metaphor
   Her hair had the movement of a river and the shiny quality of silk.
   1. fingers/sausages, *2.* boy/monkey, *3.* sun/ball, *4.* earth/globe, *5.* stars/fairy lights, *6.* ground/carpet, *7.* saw/teeth. Any comparison which makes sense – e.g. *1.* boy, *2.* reptile, *3.* giant/weed, *4.* fairy.

54 Alliteration, consonance & assonance
   a) Mavra is a **b**oxer dog. A creature **b**rave and **b**old.
   She is her owner's **p**erfect **p**et, Good with children and the vet. But when it comes to **s**it, or **s**tay,
   She never does it right away, She'd rather **s**tray than **s**tay.
   b) The surfers in their youth and pr**ide**, curl and sw**irl** and r**ide** the t**ide**. The music's b**eau**ty s**oo**thed the pupil's mind. The wind and waves s**oa**red and r**oa**red.
   c) He made a j**est**. It was a t**est**. To see if w**it** and mirth and joy, Would waken up the stricken boy, From his deep and endless r**est**.

55 Onomatopoeia
   1. crashed, *2.* bashed/buffeted, *3.* shrieked, *4.* bang, *5.* hissed, *6.* rumbled, *7.* buzzed, *8.* growled.
   Suggested responses: *1.* crunch, *2.* crash, *3.* bong, *4.* gurgle, *5.* roar, *6.* swish, *7.* whirr, *8.* buzz.

56 Personification
   1. smiling. *2.* sleeping, *3.* living, *4.* dancing, *5.* singing, *6.* whispering, *7.* gossiping, *8.* winking, *9.* stalking, *10.* speaking.
   Accept any reasonable explanation of the personification.

57 Synonyms & antonyms
   happy – merry, joyful, glad, jovial, etc. *inexpensive* – cheap, bargain, reduced, discounted, etc. *hidden* – secret, unseen, covered, masked, etc. *enormous* – huge, massive, gigantic, colossal, etc. *instantly* – now, immediately, etc. *comfortable* – cosy, snug, homely, etc. *pretty* – attractive, lovely, personable, etc. *friend* – companion, crony, mate, etc.
   Antonyms: irreversible, painless, uncertain.

58 Homographs/homonyms Teacher judgement required.

59 Homophones *1.* hall, *2.* waste. *3.* court, *4.* raw, *5.* idle, *6.* veil, *7.* passed, *8.* sure, *9.* flour, *10.* stayed, *11.* scene, *12.* stationary, *13.* whether, *14,* bore.
   peal, missed, leak, past, sum, bear, whether, sauce, broach, isle, beer, bridal, ball, ascent, pause, sleigh, stake, urn, turn.

60 Colloquial expressions Teacher judgement required.

61 Cliché & pun *1.* brute strength and ignorance, *2.* money grows on trees, *3.* he would say that, wouldn't he, *4.* right as rain, *5.* It's all one to me, *6.* nobody can cook like his mother, *7.* Hello… What have we here? *8.* Boys will be boys, *9.* no smoke without fire, *10.* six of one and half a dozen of the other.
   1. Bean, *2.* soul, *3.* Ding, Dong, *4.* fisherman, *5.* waist, *6.* plumber.

62 Rhyme & rhythm car – *far, tar, bar, star,* mouse – *house, louse, souse.* dangle – *wangle, wrangle, mangle.* head – *lead, bed, said.* Fear – *dear, leer, steer.*

63 Repetition & exaggeration Teacher judgement required to assess accuracy of responses.

64 Imported language *1.* encore, *2.* en masse, *3.* status quo, *4.* en route, *5.* Au revoir, *6.* faux pas, *7.* post mortem, *8.* ad infinitum, *9.* gourmet, *10.* curriculum vitae, *11.* fait accompli, *12.* ad lib.

65 Standard & non-standard English Teacher judgement required.

Tests

Test 1/3: Sentences
    a) 2S, 3C, 4S, 5X, 6X, 8C, 9X,10S
    b) A simple sentence contains a subject and a verb. *Example:* The **cat sat** on the mat.
    c) A compound sentence contains two simple sentences or clauses joined together by a conjunction.
        Example: I have to earn my pocket money **because** my parents say it is good for me.
    d) A complex sentence has one main clause and one or more subordinate clauses.
        Example: **The burglar was a silly man**, *he left his fingerprints at the scene of the crime* and *the police caught him easily.*

Test 4: Interrogative & imperative
    a) *1.* Im, *2.* In, *3.* In, *4.* Im, *5.* In, *6.* Im, *7.* In, *8.* In, *9.* Im, *10.* Im
    b) Interrogative = Question.
    c) Imperative = Command

Test 5/6: Conjunctions & connectives
    a) *1.* but, *2.* and, *3.* although, *4.* and, *5.* but.
    b) *1.* because, *2.* however, *3.* but/although, *4.* and.
    c) Connectives are used to join subordinate clauses to the main clause.
    d) even though, but, because, either, or, and, not only, but also.

Test 7: Phrase/Clause
    a) A phrase is a group of words which have neither their own verb nor make sense on their own.
    b) A clause occurs within a sentence, has its own verb and makes sense on its own.
    c) *1.* on Pancake Tuesday, *2.* a shaggy mongrel, *3.* in the school library, *4.* my favourite animals, *5.* with a snarl of rage.
    d) *1.* which were built of old stone, *2.* who had the Taj Mahal built, *3.* which took twenty-two years to build, *4.* smiling in delight, *5.* when the conductor gave her a nod.

Test 8/11: Nouns
    a) *1.*   A swarm (**D**) of bees (**C**) was flying in the direction of the school. (**C**)
        2.   An onion (**C**) is a very useful ingredient (**D**) in many different types of dish.
        3.   'Hatred (**A**) can be a very destructive emotion (**A**),' said the Bishop. (**C**)
        4.   Susan (**P**) and Graham (**P**) often go to the cinema (**C**) to see the latest film. (**C**)
        5.   A dog (**C**) can be an interesting and faithful friend. (**C**)
        6.   The herd (**D**) was grazing peacefully in the sunshine. (**A**)
        7.   Brian (**P**) built the new wall (**C**) from old bricks. (**C**)
        8.   My favourite game (**A**) is table tennis. (**C**)
        9.   'Please will you set the table?' (**C**) Yasmin (**P**) asked.
        10. You should try to have patience (**A**) and not lose your temper (**A**) so often.
    b) *Common:* dog, pencil, lady
        Proper: Peter, London, Atlantic Ocean
        Abstract: love, work, kindness
        Collective: swarm, herd, shoal

Test 12/13: Pronouns
    a) See Worksheets 12 and 13 for possible answers to *1. – 7.*
    b) He, you, I, you, you, I, you, you, my, my, your, mine, your, my, your, your, my, I.

Test 14: Singular & plural
- **a)** *1.* computers, were, games. *2.* children, they, monkeys, trees. *3.* men, their, umbrellas, winds. *4.* They, countries, their, holidays. *5.* They, sweets, chocolates. *6.* Thieves, houses, televisions, videos. *7.* Mice, were, houses. *8.* paintings, were, artists.
- **b)** *1.* mice, *2.* houses, *3.* dice, *4.* salmon, *5.* children, *6.* oxen.

Test 15/17: Adjectives
- **a) Adjectives – describing**
  popular, two, sizzling, welcome, bright blue, Beautiful, tanned, white sun-, loud pop, huge, beach, few, sun-tan, bronzed, harmful, burning, Laughing, shallow turquoise, anxious, holiday, pure.
- **b) Adjectives – comparing**
  1. taller, *2.* fastest, *3.* worse, *4.* more beautiful, *5.* most difficult.
- **c) Adjectives – possessive**
  their, my, mine, theirs, My, your, my, its, Our, his, her, my, mine, my.

Test 20: Auxiliary verbs
- **a)** *1.* am, *2.* are, *3.* have, *4.* were, *5.* are, *6.* had, *7.* were, *8.* might, *9.* ought, *10.* should.
- **b)** *1.* Do… *2.* Does… *3.* doesn't… *4.* Don't… *5.* doesn't… *6.* done… *7.* Did… *8.* didn't… *9.* had to do… *10.* doesn't do…

Test 22: Active & passive voices – verbs
- **a)** *1.* The garden was dug (**P**) by a local gardener. *2.* I always dig (**A**) the garden myself. *3.* They fed (**A**) the dog raw meat. *4.* The cover had been made (**P**) by hand. *5.* The book had been read (**P**) many times.
- **b) Passive to active.** *1.* A very good musician played the keyboard. *2.* A supply teacher taught the lesson. *3.* A boy and his sister flew the kite. *4.* The cook made the omelet. *5.* The pilot flew the plane.
- **c) Active to passive.** *1.* The bed was made by Peter. *2.* The family was frightened by the ghost. *3.* The letter was written by Jane. *4.* The strawberries were picked by Mum. *5.* The car was mended by Dad.

Test 23/31: Verbs – tense

a)

	to play		to be
Present	I play	*Present*	he/she/it is
Past	I played	*Past*	he/she/it was
Future	I will play	*Future*	he/she/it will be

- **b)** I **am** singing. **c)** we **were** digging. **d)** He/she/it **will/shall be** diving.
- **e)** He/she/it **has** built. **f)** You **have been** building.
- **g) I had done** too much homework. In fact, it seemed as if I **had been doing** too much homework for weeks. The exams **had finished** now thank goodness. If **I had revised** properly all term, I wouldn't **have been staying** up to all hours trying to catch up. **I had been** a fool but **I have been trying** hard to make up for my past laziness.
- **h)** I **shall have finished** my tea by the time you are changed. You **will have been getting ready** to go out for two hours. I **will have eaten**, washed up and I **shall** still **have taken** less time than you've taken. It's a good job we're not in a hurry.

Test 32/3: Adverbs
- **a)** An adverb adds to the meaning of a verb.
- **b)** Any adverb which is placed accurately under each heading. Note the examples.

time	place	manner	frequency	degree
now	up	sharply	never	very
later	inside	forcefully	rarely	slightly

- **c)** madly, breathlessly, really, disapprovingly, frighteningly, punctually, hastily.
- **d)** very/really, patiently, quickly/swiftly, already, comfortably, slowly/hungrily, briefly/hurriedly, absolutely, angrily.

Test 34: Adverbs – comparative & superlative
- **a)** faster/fastest, harder/hardest, more slowly/most slowly, more loud/most loudly.
- **b)** *1.* earlier, *2.* more neatly, *3.* most quickly, *4.* most loudly, *5.* highest, *6.* faster, *7.* most tightly, *8.* better.
- **c)** *1.* worse, *2.* the loudest, *3.* best. *4.* best.

Test 36/7: Pronouns
- **a)** *1.* whom, *2.* who, *3.* which, *4.* whom, *5.* that.
- **b)** Relates one part of a sentence to another.
- **c)** *1.* I, *2.* me, *3.* me, *4.* me, *5.* I.
- **d)** *1.* He/She, *2.* we, *3.* wants, *4.* were, *5.* They/We.

Test 38: Prepositions

a) A preposition shows the position of one thing in relation to another in a sentence.

b) *1.* around, *2.* under, *3.* on, *4.* after, *5.* through, *6.* beside, *7.* under, *8.* before, *9.* behind, *10.* against.

Test 39/40: Capital letters & full stops

a) James, Easter, America, Cinderella, Europe, Eiffel Tower, Euston Station, Corfu

b) We, London, Wembley Stadium, They, I, Romeo and Juliet.

c) It was a beautiful day. **M**um and **D**ad decided to take the whole family, including dogs, to **B**lackpool to spend the day on the beach. **A**s soon as we left, there was a loud bang.

'**O**h … ' said **D**ad. '**W**e've had a puncture.' **D**ad called the garage because he couldn't undo the wheel nuts. **H**e was mad. It took two hours for someone to arrive and change the wheel. **W**e set off again. **I**t started to rain – no, to pour. **T**he rain was so heavy **D**ad had to stop the car. **W**hat a day out!

Test 41: Commas

a) *1.* I would like to go out tonight, if you come as well. *2.* They are good friends, even though they often argue. *3.* The dog, usually well behaved, started barking madly. *4.* You can go to the ball, Cinderella, providing you are home by midnight. *5.* My favourite foods are chicken, fish, cherries, peaches and good bread. *6.* If we decided not to go running, then we could swim. *7.* Walking is good for you, so we are told. *8.* The surgery had appointments at five o'clock, five fifteen, five thirty or a quarter to six. *9.* The cut was deep, bleeding heavily, covered in mud and I was sure in need of stitches. *10.* The old man, of whom many tales were told, had an interesting face.

b) 3,096 – 24,300 – 103,863 – 8,974,320 – 56,743,200,109

c) To separate out items in a list.

d) To help us to make sense of sentences when there are several parts to them.

e) To separate subordinate clauses from the main clause.

Test 42/3: Apostrophe of omission & possession

a) I am, you will, he is, is not, she is, we would, of the clock, I have.

b) wouldn't, don't, they'd, who's, you've, we'll, shouldn't, I won't.

c) Joanna's, Peter's, James', men's, Rosa's, children's.

d) It's, I'm, it's James', We're, We'll, James', couldn't, anyone's, They'd, we'll, we're, Mary's, family's, She's, she's.

Test 44: Exclamation & question marks

a) *1.* ?, Q, *2.* ., S, *3.* !, x, *4.* ?, Q, *5.* ., S, *6.* !, x, *7.* ., S, *8.* ?, Q.

b) 'Help!' The girl cried as loudly as she could. Would someone arrive in time to save her?

'Help me!' She screamed in fear. The water was rising fast. Where was her brother?

'Ouch!' Dad exclaimed as the hammer hit his thumb for the second time. 'Why does it always happen to me? I must be the most unlucky do-it-yourself person in the world,' he muttered.

'Oh no!' The shelf he was fixing started to tilt. 'Will somebody please come and hold this up?' he yelled crossly.

'Why do you always make such a fuss when you do any little job?' cried Mum.

'Fuss! Fuss! What do you mean, fuss?' Dad replied.

'It is more a question of do-it-ourselves than do-it-yourself, isn't it?' said Mum.

Test 46: Hyphen/dash

a) half-baked, father-in-law, mother-in-law, half-hour, semi-detached, re-form, half-hearted, second-hand, Pre-school, short-term, non-stick, re-cover.

b) *1.* There was no need for proof – he was a thief in the minds of the crowd.

2. All of them – along with their belongings – were herded into a room.

3. The weather was bad – not unusual in this part of the world – and the ferry was cancelled.

4. Johnson – a harsh but fair judge – was in court that day.

5. The furniture – covered in dust sheets – showed that the house was not occupied.

6. Enough of all this talk – come in and have something to eat.

7. Tom made the excuse – as if he needed one – that he was growing and needed lots to eat.

8. The material – a beautiful heavy silk – fell to the ground in graceful folds.

9. The whole team – large, small, old, young, fat, thin – jumped with joy when they won.

10. Information – secret information – has been stolen.

Test 47/8: Speech marks, direct & indirect speech

a) 'Where are you, John?' Mum called. 'It's your turn to wash up. You promised to share the jobs with Rosa if I bought you a computer.'

'Coming, Mum,' John answered without enthusiasm. 'I'll just finish this game.'

'John, I called you half an hour ago,' Mum shouted angrily. 'If you can't keep your side of the bargain, that computer is going.'

'I give in,' John said and trailed into the kitchen. Mums always win in the end.

◆◆◆◆◆◆◆◆◆◆◆◆◆◆◆◆◆◆◆◆◆◆◆◆◆◆◆◆◆◆

'Hello. How are you?' asked my uncle.

'Fed up and hard up,' I replied.

'The trouble with you young people ...,' he continued, listing the weaknesses of modern youth.

'I'm sure you always spent your money wisely,' I said to him.

'I bet you've never had the fun I've had spending mine unwisely,' I said to myself.

b) *1.* D, *2.* I, *3.* D, *4.* I, *5.* I, *6.* I, *7.* D, *8.* D, *9.* I, *10.* D.

Test 49: Semi-colon/colon

a) *1.* Some pupils are keen to make progress; others prefer to make chaos.

2. The match was important; everyone knew that.

3. He would need shirt, shorts and boots; food for the journey; money for his ticket.

b) We decided to form a gang. We had several lots of enemies: the Clongs, the Wets and the Misfits. We had to choose the members of our gang from the following list: Mary, Jasmin, Clive, Ranjit and Rohima. Bonkers, our leader, quoted the saying: 'You can't make a silk purse out of a sow's ear.' The others weren't impressed: they didn't know what it meant.

c) *1.* The dancer was known as Flight; a name which suited her perfectly.

2. In many films, the hero disappears into the sunset; the music fades away.

3. I love coffee: my sister prefers water.

4. The recipe is very rich and requires these ingredients: a dozen eggs, 500g of chocolate, 250g butter, 250g sugar and half a litre of cream.

5. Mum's favourite quotation: 'Fortune favours the brave.'

6. As a teacher I had one main aim: for my class to be the happiest in the school.

7. I was late so I called a taxi; the taxi rank is just around the corner from my house.

8. I was an actor working so hard I had no time for fun: how could I change things?

9. My mother said to herself: I will change ....

10. For next term we need to order the following: ten packs of pens, six reams ....

Test 50: Paragraphing

a) See sheet 50

b) day? || You.   important. || Think.